IN SEARCH OF BUSINESS VALUE

Also by Robert McDowell and William L. Simon

Driving Digital

IN SEARCH OF BUSINESS VALUE

Insuring a Return on Your Technology Investment

Robert L. McDowell
Vice President, Microsoft Corporation

and William L. Simon

Foreword by Jeff Raikes
Group Vice President, Microsoft Corporation

SelectBooks, Inc.

In Search of Business Value: Ensuring a Return on Your
Technology Investment
Copyright ©2004 by Robert L. McDowell and William L. Simon
All rights reserved.
This edition published by SelectBooks, Inc., New York, New York

First Edition
ISBN 1-59079-062-6

Author cover photo by Linda Lawrence and Phototime

Library of Congress Cataloging-in-Publication Data
McDowell, Robert L., 1945-
  In search of business value : ensuring a return on your
technology investment / Robert McDowell and William L. Simon.–
1st ed.
      p. cm.
  Includes index.
  ISBN 1-59079-062-6 (hardcover : alk. paper)
  1. Information technology–Management. 2. Technological
innovations–Management. 3. Organizational effectiveness.
  4. Competition.
I. Simon, William L., 1930- II. Title.
HD30.2.M3954 2004
004'.068–dc22

                    2004012619

Manufactured in the United States of America

              10 9 8 7 6 5 4 3 2 1

To Lissa

and Arynne

Contents

Foreword   ix

Introduction: The Promise of Technology   xi

The Cast of Characters   xv

PART ONE: The Role of IT   1

Chapter 1   Achieving Business Value is a Leadership Issue, Not a Technology Issue   3

Chapter 2   Anybody Buying Technology Only for the Sake of the Technology Just Doesn't Get It   21

Chapter 3   You're Using Technology in Support of Business Processes—Right?   43

PART TWO: Making the Business Case for Technology   57

Chapter 4   Making the Business Case for Technology, I: Justifying the Technology Spend   59

Chapter 5   Making the Business Case for Technology, II: Demonstrating Value After the Fact   79

PART THREE: Governance, Culture, and the Challenge of Running IT   95

Chapter 6   Let's Give Governance a Chance   97

Chapter 7   "The Beatings Will Continue Until the Culture
             Improves"   113

Chapter 8   Why Aren't You Using the "Ruby Slippers"
             Approach?   129

PART FOUR: Controversy and Miscellany   151

Chapter 9   "Everything That Can Be Invented Has Already Been
             Invented"   153

Chapter 10   ...And in Conclusion: A Collection of Other Ideas
             and Viewpoints   167

Profiles   191
Acknowledgments   207
Appendix   211
Glossary   213
Index   215

Foreword

Jeff Raikes

Group Vice President, Microsoft Corporation

The day isn't too far off when the head of every company, and the people running every major unit within the enterprise, will be people who grew up with the computer—folks who played with computers as kids, used them all the way through school, and learned to look at them as a valuable tool for getting things done.

When that day comes, a book like this one won't be necessary. Nobody will need it, nobody will want to read it. Well, we're not there yet. Walk through the executive suites and the offices of any company today and you'll still find people who look on the computer with a bit of suspicion and mistrust.

At Microsoft we've always been lucky about this. We never had trouble finding people who saw technology as useful, worthwhile, and cool; they came knocking at our door from the very first, and they still do. But even with that advantage, we still miss the boat on some issues.

Bill Gates once asked Steve Ballmer how many printed forms Microsoft uses, figuring the answer might be something like twenty or twenty-five. The number turned out to be in the hundreds. We were selling technology to help other companies be efficient, but we were drowning under the weight of our own paper.

Even though we have made a great deal of progress since then, the experience sticks in my mind as an example. We came to recognize that each form represents a process, and instead of just getting rid of paper forms, we began to take a hard look at some of our processes. We were doing purchasing much like other companies, but the process was out of whack, and discovering that led us to develop a new approach to how we interface with our vendor community and how our employees place orders for the things they need. The outcome: we've changed how the Purchasing Department works, with employees now ordering most things self-service, and we dramatically reduced the cost of purchasing—by 70 percent.

This book is full of such stories. It comes as a follow-up to *Driving Digital,* an earlier volume by the same two authors. For that book and this new one, Bob McDowell writes with the authority and experience of a Microsoft vice president who is a prime contact for us with corporate leaders, technology executives, and board chairmen around the world, and brings back to the company information about their concerns and their needs in technology. The experience puts Bob in the forefront of understanding how businesses are successfully gaining benefits from technology, and where they're missing the boat.

Inspired by the feedback from readers of the previous book, Bob and best-selling author Bill Simon set out to pull together key ideas from leaders of businesses and IT organizations, in their own words, about how best to achieve the maximum business value from technology. Because in today's world, that's the name of the game, a major determinate of corporate success.

In the 1980's and 90's, whenever the words "new" and "technology" came together, that seemed enough justification in itself for approving technology budgets. In this new millennium, with technology costs adding up to a major item in every company's financial plan, just being new isn't enough any more. I've personally heard plenty of complaints from top company executives and IT frontrunners uncomfortable about whether their IT expenditures are truly bringing business value.

With IT spend taking such a big chunk of the corporate budget, the question of how to be sure you achieve business value from technology has never been of greater urgency. It's the underlying question explored in this book, offering insight from both corporate leaders and leaders of IT.

How to make sure you get value for your technology dollars is the central theme of this book. For today's business leaders, I think there are few issues more important.

Introduction: The Promise of Technology

Outside your frosty window, an ice storm rages. Weighty fingers of frozen water droop from tree branches bent low in exhaustion. Enough of this! You're ready for a vacation where the hot sun is brilliant and waiting to tint your skin to a golden glow.

So you punch in the phone number of JetBlue Airways, and while on hold wonder if the Call Center you're being connected to is in some dingy city suffering a weather blitz of an icy sort similar to your own. You imagine someone trapped in a little cubicle and wired to earphones while you describe your trip to a sandy cove. You wonder whether the reservation clerk you speak to will be envious of your escape to the warmth.

But no. This JetBlue reservation clerk is in her own cozy home, perhaps with a pot of soothing herbal tea brewing and fuzzy slippers on her feet while she types in the data for your flight. At the time of this writing, JetBlue has some five hundred of these snug reservation clerks, each working from her or his own living room or rec room or kitchen. Your image of a vast room with cramped, impersonal cubicles is wrong, all wrong.

Can such a radically humanistic idea pay off? You bet it can, and it does. It's a contributing factor to this surprising statistic: the average cost of Information Technology as a share of revenues in the airline industry is about 5 percent. Miracle of miracles—according to former Chief Information Officer Jeff Cohen, JetBlue spends 1.4 percent, less than one-third as much.

The JetBlue story raises a series of pertinent and timely questions, such as: How can an organization—how can *your* organization—wring business value from technology? What are the governing principles? What are the 'best practices'?

Old Needs Still Not Addressed

Since the dawn of the high-tech era, there can't be many other issues that have been studied, examined, discussed, and argued about more than the hot-button issue of whether a company can gain competitive advantage from technology. A *Fortune* magazine cover story from, incredibly, 1986, carried the title "The Puny Payoff from Office Computers." The article pointed out that "managers and consultants who have studied the problem offer several explanations for why computers have not improved white-collar productivity," and went on to identify a number of issues such as the need to change workflows—issues that Bill Simon and I heard nearly twenty years later from the leaders interviewed for this book.

The eminent Paul A. Strassmann sounded the same alarm in 1988, in a book he co-edited entitled *Measuring Business Value of Information Technologies* (Paul A. Strassmann, et al, ICIT Press, 1988). Again, the conclusions of the book cite a list of issues, almost all of which you will find in these pages. It all has the ring of a Polonius type, or some elderly uncle in Dickens who repeats the same cautions and warnings over and over.

And the issue was stirred up yet again by a now-notorious article in the May 2003 issue of the *Harvard Business Review,* carrying the provocative title, "IT Doesn't Matter." In it, author Nicholas Carr argued that IT has become a commodity and can no longer provide competitive advantage. I agree with many of his points; much of his criticism is on target, and in fact similar concerns have been raised by many voices virtually since the time computers began to be used in business.

Still, that single *HBR* article stirred enough controversy to reveal this as a question people can still become heated about. I take strong exception to many of his points, as do lots of the people interviewed for this book; in Chapter 9, you'll find an intriguing and enlightening diversity of views on the subject.

I wondered what catalyst had launched this question to be of such heightened interest at this particular juncture in business history. Three elements, I believe, can be held responsible—three cataclysmic events in the years around the turn of the 20th century that shook corporate America (and corporate everywhere).

First we saw the big growth in IT spending as the Nineties closed because of the Y2K scare. Heaps of money got spent to make sure the lights wouldn't shut off and the wheels of industry wouldn't stop turning at midnight on New Year's Eve. A great many IT investments were made without the usual discipline of scrutiny or projections of anticipated cost benefits because the goal was simply to avert disaster.

We made it through. Now that issue is off the burner and it's a long time until we get to Y3K.

The second factor was the dot.com implosion. Of course, it wasn't the Internet that imploded. Rather it was a new math that described value to a company by multiplying earnings-that-don't-yet-exist by a factor of 250 or some such. (While many of those companies may well have deserved to disappear, the Internet itself remains alive and kicking, and a driver for a goodly chunk of the IT expenditures of most companies.)

And the third factor was the tragedy of 9/11, a horrific day that brought about many changes. September 11th became a catalyst that helped further drive down the stock market and made people everywhere face some harsh economic realities—tough times that many younger people in business had never seen before. With the stock market stained by red ink and businesses having to cut back dramatically, the focus on any expenditure—IT spends very much included—meant that business leaders began to face hard-core payback issues with a level of intensity that hadn't existed before.

The business climate has changed. In today's climate, these same issues that people have been raising over and over through the years about the benefits of technology can no longer be ignored. The subject has taken on a new urgency. It's time to stop talking about all this and start taking new steps to *do* something about it. And that's the goal of this book.

About this Book

In our previous work, *Driving Digital,* Bill Simon and I explored what distinguished one company from another in the effective use of technology. This book extends the ideas presented there with a new focus—one that is, or should be, a matter of high concern for all companies and organizations in today's digital world: exploring best-practice techniques for wringing the maximum business value out of every technology dollar.

I wanted to write this book in hope of finally bringing clarity and closure to the questions about the critical success factors for realizing business value from technology. Together, Bill and I reached out to a wide diversity of business leaders and managers in a variety of industries, asking for personal experiences, views and opinions, stories of successes and failures that would shed light on the subject and benefit us all by learning from one another. The stories taken together add up to a picture of how businesses can get the best bang for every IT buck spent.

The overarching message is simple: If you want value from technology investments, there are certain things you must do. If you aren't taking these essential steps, then I think pointing to the cost of technology or the failings of technology as the only source of your organization's problems is just plain wrong.

Let's face reality here: We're looking at an issue that's not for the most part a technology failure. Sure, we all see plenty of examples of technology being overhyped, technology misused, and projects that fail to deliver promised results. What we're seeing in case after case is not a technology failure, it's a management failure.

This book carries the message that IT departments have become a catalyst for leading management to recognize a new potential: the potential for *innovating* with technology. The participants argue that the obligation is in the hands of the business leader—because this kind of innovation usually involves culture change. And that means the change will be neither comfortable nor easy. But as you will see, in the view of those interviewed here, change that leads to innovation from technology, as well as change inspired by technology, prove to be more than worth the effort.

That's part of what awaits you in the following pages. Read, enjoy, and learn—and stay on the lookout for our next book.

The Cast of Characters

People Whose Words Make Up the Heart of this Book

Note: A brief bio of each of these people, and some details on their company or organization, are presented in the Profiles section at the end of the book.

Lawrence Baxter, Chief eCommerce Officer, Wachovia Corporation

Dave Borland, Deputy Chief Information Officer, U.S. Army

Lt. General Steven Boutelle, CIO, U.S. Army

Joe Capps, Director, Enterprise Systems Technology Activity, U.S. Army

Dave Clementz, CIO, ChevronTexaco Corporation

Avery Cloud, CIO, Integris Health

Jeff Cohen, former CIO, JetBlue Airways Corporation

Susan Conway, Industry Director, Information Work Productivity Council, Microsoft Corporation

Craig Cuyar, CIO, CommonHealth

David Farquhar, Chief Operating Officer, Interactive University, Edinburgh, Scotland

Patricia Gabow, MD, Chief Executive Officer, Denver Health

Richard Greenwood, CIO, Residential Capital Group, GMAC-RFC

Jeremy V. Gross, Executive Vice President and CIO, Washington Mutual, Inc.

Steven Hankins, CFO, Tyson Foods, Inc.

Stan Hupfeld, CEO, Integris Health, Inc.

S. Kregg Jodie, CIO, Mary Kay Inc.

Archie Kane, Group Executive Director, Lloyds TSB Group plc, London, England (Lloyds Bank)

Professor Roy Leitch, Chief Executive, Interactive University, Edinburgh, Scotland

Lic. Jazmín Loaiza, Chief Manager for Systems, Pemex Oil, Mexico

Eric Meslow, Founder and CEO, Timbercon, Inc.

Rachelle Mileur, Director of eCommerce Systems Development, Airborne Express

Gary Moore, Senior Vice President, Cisco Systems, Inc.

John Rootenberg, MD, Director of Information Technology and Services for Clinical Research, the University of California, San Francisco, and Director of Informatics for the university's Department of Neurology

Prof. Lee Schlenker, École de Management (The Graduate School of Management), Lyon, France

Karen Settle, Founder and President, Keystone Marketing, Inc.

Roger Smith, Senior Vice President, Marsh Inc.

Terry Szpak, Founder, Telesystems West

Carla von Bernewitz, Director, Enterprise Integration Oversight Office, U.S. Army

David Wilson, President, East Industries

PART ONE

The Role of IT

1

Achieving Business Value is a Leadership Issue, Not a Technology Issue

> We got the entire management team enabled very, very quickly, in about thirty days, to the point of being able to use all the basic tools. From that point on, the rest of the corporation has just followed from there—within six months.
>
> — Jerry Gross, *CIO, Washington Mutual*

How does any company set itself up for wringing the greatest business value from its technology spend? Ultimately it's not the hardware and software decisions that matter most; it's a question of leadership.

The level of engagement of business leaders and Information Technologies leaders determines whether the system ultimately serves as a catalyst for delivering real business value. What kind of "engagement"? One key issue: are senior managers using technology themselves; this is an aspect of what at Microsoft we call "eating our own dog food." It's the example of every military organization—the commander who sits on the hilltop issuing orders doesn't get the same results as the commander who leads his troops into battle.

In the same way, realizing business value from technology is a challenge both to the leader of the technology organization and, as well and maybe even more important, to the leader of the enterprise.

Achieving a Sense of Technology

A lot of people might say that Jerry Gross (rhymes with 'floss') has it easy. As the Chief Information Officer at Washington Mutual for the past three years, Jerry is the technology wrangler for a bank that

3

has been in business since the 1890's and currently holds a mortgage portfolio of some $700 billion, which you've got to admit is an impressive number. And he's blessed with a boss who has learned to appreciate the role of technology—

> Like many corporate leaders, Kerry Killinger, our Chief Executive Officer and Chairman, has come to see the incredible value that technology can bring to our business.

How does a CIO get a CEO to fully appreciate both technology's strategic benefit and its contribution to the bottom line? Jerry Gross explains—

> Establishing credibility right from the get-go is fundamental. Like many companies, Washington Mutual had for years used monolithic outsourcing agreements for things like desktop support and telecom. As the organization grew from a small regional bank to a large bank with a national presence, this became an expensive way to handle the outsourcing. One of the first things our team did when we came on board was to restructure those agreements to take advantage of the bargaining power associated with the larger presence of the company—resulting in a savings of millions of dollars. So from a cost perspective, credibility was established with a numbers-driven CEO right from the start.

Another factor that Jerry pointed to was a culture change in IT—

> The IT organization was going through a lot of change. The type of people we began bringing in were different—they didn't just have the technical knowledge; they could also talk about technology so that non-technical people could understand.

Jerry also came up with the idea of using what he terms "quick-hit deliverables" so everyone would constantly see positive things coming from IT—

> I made sure that every thirty days we were delivering something people could feel and touch. We had our twelve-month objectives and our six-month objectives, but every single month I saw to it that we had another quick hit. One month it was remote access to the Intranet, another it was VPN (Virtual Private Network).

And then we publicized that, not to beat our chests, but to just say, 'Hey, everybody—here's what's now available.'

I also built out a communication group. Only three people, but their job was to make sure people understood that these changes were happening and how it would benefit them. And employees started becoming advocates for these changes. Communication is a huge part of a cultural change.

But one other approach Jerry used to bring about greater comfort with technology turned out to be the most significant of all—

I went into the Chairman's office one day and sat down with him and said, 'Look, this stuff is neat, fun, and cool. And it's practical.' I showed him how to use it. Like with so many people, that's all it really took to get him excited with the technology.

Then very quickly we got a pilot program going; this is part of the innovation effort I wanted to talk about, and why it's so critical.

But I sat down with him and said, "Here's what wireless messaging is, here's what's possible with it." Then I gave him and the rest of our executive team a tremendous amount of support. The bank had never had dedicated technology support for the top executives. We got a group of young, smart, very outgoing, friendly people from IT to support the top management team.

We got the entire management team enabled very, very quickly, in about thirty days, to the point of being able to use all the basic tools. From that point on, the rest of the corporation has just followed from there—within six months.

That's a powerful lesson for any company with employees who are dragging their feet about adopting technology. You've got to get your top executive team over their individual discomforts...but once you do, they'll set the example for the rest of the company. The new attitudes will trickle down:

After only about six months, WaMu people began to have a feeling that there was a new focus, a service-oriented focus, that was being made possible by technology. They sensed that the IT people really cared about delivering technology services.

So the change in attitude came from a combination of elements—cost savings, a stream of new things coming from IT, and good communications to make sure everyone in the company knew about available technology. It came from culture change of the leadership, and culture change in IT.

Bottom Up or Top Down?

It's almost a cliché in business that change doesn't happen unless it's supported from the top. You'd probably be hard pressed to find three business executives who don't already subscribe to this notion. That makes it all the more difficult for technology, since commands for change are not likely to issue forth from the office of an executive who still thinks of technology as bits and bytes.

The U.S. Army's Director of Enterprise Integration Oversight, Carla von Bernewitz, offered an interesting perspective on this—

> I've done a lot of research into how organizations put new systems into place, and very often you'll find that a good idea gets started in a particular business unit or a particular functional area, whether the good idea is for a system, program, or some sort of organizational change. And it's great for that particular unit, but then it stays within the walls of that unit and never goes any further.
>
> So you can have efforts that don't come from the very top of the organization, but they still have to be sponsored from the top of the organization that is adopting the change—let's say Finance, for example, or HR—in order to be effective.
>
> But if you're going to see the true impact across the entire enterprise, then it has to come from the very top.

Making Sure the Executives Use Technology Themselves

When business leaders don't grasp the value and strategic significance of technology, the burden falls on the CIO to get the message across.

One CIO who addressed this subject for us was Rick Greenwood. His organization, the Residential Capital Group of Residential Funding Corporation, is a wholly owned subsidiary of General

Motors Acceptance Corporation (GMAC). Rick spoke of the need to make sure that the top leaders of the organization are acquiring "an appetite for technology." To subtly push in that direction within his own organization, Rick began organizing a technology refresher once or twice a year:

> We show them new technology, like wireless. I go in to talk to one of them, and he can see that I'm looking at e-mails on some kind of handheld, for example. With new technology always coming forward and bringing new capabilities, we give them ideas of the kind of R&D projects that we could do within their environment.
>
> Last spring we focused on wireless technology, because they all had cell phones, and some had Blackberries, and you could see there was some dependence on it. So we spent time with them, talking about what would be a strategy for going forward? How could they keep in touch with each other better? And that was quite effective.
>
> I was trying to convey that they have to have some technology savvy, and I dropped some ideas of how they can use technology or what technology can bring. They don't need to understand the 'how' of it, but they need to understand what the capabilities are.

Just when it sounds as if he's made real headway, Rick puts another spin on the topic, and then shows the kind of determination that should be part of the job description for any CIO—

> Every now and again my boss, the president of the Residential Capital Group, will still tell me that it's a challenge for him to understand what capabilities we're trying to achieve, or why we're pursuing a particular technology. And I'm aware that a piece of technology for me can be just a black box for him.
>
> But that's my job as a CIO: to him, IT should not be a black box. You have to keep explaining, breaking it down in business terms and business value. Because if you let your leadership keep on accepting IT as a black box, you're in trouble.

CIO and CFO as a Team

Not every company has a CEO who takes a hands-on approach to technology decisions. We found one instance of this at Common-

Health, the world's largest healthcare communications organization. Based in New Jersey, the firm is a holding company for a con-
glomerate of firms providing advertising, marketing, medical education, and other service for the healthcare industry. Craig Cuyar
holds the titles of senior vice president and CIO—

> The final sales job, if you will, is [that of] the CFO. And then
> ultimately the numbers that we predict will be required for the
> implementation in terms of capital and operating expenses
> need to be fed back into the organizational budget, revenue
> projections, and so forth.
>
> And it will ultimately be the CFO who says, 'Yes, we can do
> this,' or, 'No, we can't do this now. Can you move it out six
> months?'
>
> Myself and the CFO both report to the CEO, and if we can
> go with a combined argument for a particular technology or
> system implementation, it's a fairly easy conversation. Our CEO
> recognizes the need to infuse technology throughout our busi-
> ness units as one method to increase productivity and remain
> competitive in our industry. As such, he readily supports our
> combined decisions and becomes fully committed to the effort.

Who better than the CFO to bless a benefits calculation for a
technology spend? Any CEO can count himself fortunate if he has
a CFO who can be counted on in situations like this. Just as long as
the arrangement isn't a screen that the CEO uses to insulate himself
from being involved in technology decisions.

Technology as Strategy

One of the critical issues here, an issue that's been talked about for
years, is the need to establish a tight connection tying technology
planning into business planning. If the starting point is the business
priority, the first thing you want to do from an IT perspective is to
dig in and figure out where IT has the potential for providing the
greatest support to the top business priorities.

Many companies don't discipline themselves in this regard. We
could all do well to take a leaf from the experience of the Mary Kay
organization, as described by its CIO, Kregg Jodie:

> We came to the understanding, especially with the growth of
> the Internet, that strategically for Mary Kay Inc., it was going to

be critical to really exploit that technology and use it to communicate to sales force, which numbers more than 1.1 million people worldwide. We call them 'Independent Beauty Consultants,' and as the title suggests, they're not employees.

We saw that our goal of being able to communicate with them and motivate them could be enhanced greatly by a communication channel that would enable us to touch base with them every day. And the way that we were going to leverage the technology for this was not going to be by creating a different channel or changing the principles of our business model. Everybody on the Internet, it seemed like, was talking about maybe going directly retail. But [company founder] Mary Kay Ash had laid down the principle that we're in business for our sales force.

So how should the Internet play a role in our business model? I, and others, felt that it could be the connection point not only for completing orders, but also for communications, recognition, and marketing to our Consultants. And beyond that, even providing websites to our Consultants so that they could capitalize upon another professional marketing tool for their own customers.

This sounds like a strategic decision that would require top-level approval from the outset; that's not, in fact, how it actually happened. Kregg explained, "Strategic backing from the leadership team wasn't a big issue in the beginning because we weren't aiming to change processes, we were just duplicating the existing processes on the Internet—so it wasn't seen as much of a risk." And then, as the success of the Internet project became very visible, "Our confidence grew that this approach could become a strategic tool for Mary Kay. Once the executive team came to realize the strategic importance of the Internet, they began to view IT differently."

A Matter of Trust

People who aren't entirely comfortable with technology, or who look on IT folks just as the people you talk to when you need new computers or new networking, tend to be slow to accept the idea of a relationship of trust between themselves, on the business side, and the techno wonks. That notion was addressed by Roger Smith, a Senior Vice President of Marsh Inc., the $6 billion global risk and insurance brokerage firm—

One of the challenges we deal with is that technology is not a core business skill of an insurance broker. Not to say Marsh doesn't have employees who have that skill—we do. But people driving the business in Marsh do not have technology as their core skill. And this is nothing new at the company; it's been this way for twenty years.

Roger described bridging this gulf as a two-step process:

The first challenge is translating the business needs into a technology solution. The second is getting colleagues to trust in the translation—establishing the confidence that a technology colleague truly understands what his business colleague is trying to achieve. We work very hard at building that trust.

Having recently been through a training program at General Electric, Roger had glommed onto a phrase widely used there: "Go slow to go fast." He commented, "It's a good way of saying you should take the time for thorough due diligence, and then the results will be much better."

For instance, when we embark on a technology project, we insist that the business owner participate. That usually means at least bimonthly discussions and updates with the developers, so that everything stays on track.

What seems to happen is that the developers come up with a lot of clever added things that they think up and design into an application. For example, 'I'll give you this button on screen; you just click on it and a copy of the section will go to all your trading partners.'

But sometimes those clever additions are actually counterproductive to what the business owner wants; he or she may say, 'No, no, no, we won't want it to go to all the trading partners as a group, we need the ability to send only to an individual trading partner.'

So we prevent these kinds of issues by insisting that the business owner stay involved during the development. And that's just the best way. It's a great process.

For Roger, the chief advantage of reaching the stage when infrastructure becomes a dependable service is that the technology people, and the CIO in particular, have more time to focus on strategy:

In many ways, technology that supports our business is a lot like tap water: you expect it to be there when you turn on the faucet. I don't hear complaints about our technology department. When I go into other companies and talk to them about issues, or participate in a business roundtable, I run into a lot of complaining about IT. Nothing is perfect, but I don't hear those comments out in the field about our (headquarters) IT folks in New York.

In fact, when we had the Northeast power outage in the summer of 2003, the only down time was with a dial-in service we use when we connect remotely, not Marsh Technology—so we fared very, very well on that. I was very pleased because it showed our infrastructure management is to the point we really can treat it almost as a commodity. It's dependable, we know what to expect, we get what we expect.

So we can spend our thinking on strategy. The spend might be 80–20 [that is, 80 percent on infrastructure, 20 percent on strategic issues], but the intellectual capital is probably 80–20 the other way. And because we don't have to agonize about infrastructure—What do we need to do?—we're able instead to spend more time on questions about, 'Where should we be?' And a lot of that is focused on the customer, as it should be.

To go back to the tap water analogy, I recognize there is a lot of infrastructure that enables me to turn on the tap and get water. And, at times during our growth as a firm, the spend on infrastructure has required some balancing and some advanced planning, not only by IT but also by our business segments.

Clearly it's a good thing, a sign of maturity in IT, when most of the intellectual energy can be focused on strategic issues.

The Difficulty of Explaining IT as Strategy

In many situations, even technology infrastructure can offer strategic value to an organization—but explaining that value can pose a significant challenge. Steven Boutelle is one CIO who has found this a particular problem; his rank is Lieutenant General, his organization is the U.S. Army (one of the biggest users of technology in the world), and the people he needs to convince include top Pentagon brass and members of Congressional committees. General Boutelle told us—

If we determine that we need 400 pounds of network, how do you show that to anybody? It's easy to buy something that's tangible, that has size, weight, cube, mass. We can come in and say, 'We need three F16s,' or 'one aircraft carrier,' or 'a hundred tanks'—they can identify with that. If we have a thousand tanks, we can count them and we can put our fingers on where they are. The people with the money can find the fiscal reality against specific tangible items, so they don't have any problem with that aspect of the request.

But we still have a significant issue going to the people who do the resourcing and saying, 'I need to buy a broadband network that ties Charleston, South Carolina, with the marines in Baghdad.' And you can just see them thinking, 'Well, what does it look like?' What good would it do to say, 'Here's a picture that shows a bunch of routers in a 19-inch rack'?

This is directly parallel to what we're seeing in the private sector. It's easy to go up before the CEO and say, "Please fund this new system to make our supply operation more efficient," or whatever, "And here's the cost payback." It's a lot harder to go to the CEO and say, "I need to do a massive investment in upgrading the network." When he says, "Why?" you try to explain: "Because we can't do any of this other stuff without that in place." But you can't demonstrate it, you can't explain it the way you can explain the supply system.

What's the answer? I'll tell you what the answer is—the only answer I can see: top executives who already understand and appreciate technology well enough that they don't have to be educated every time their technology chief walks in the door. When you talk about the network, or some other expensive technology, they already understand what it is and the kind of benefits it can bring.

Even at Washington Mutual, with the understanding that CIO Jerry Gross finds from his Chairman, it's not all a rose garden. "Whether the Chairman still thinks technology is too expensive is another question. For example, we just purchased a new data center, in Dallas. And being a numbers-driven guy, he's asked 'Are you sure we need to spend all this money?'"

"Infrastructure," Gross has discovered, "is always a tough sell."

A Seat at the Table

If there's an agreement that technology is of potential strategic value to an organization, it makes sense that the head of IT needs to be given a chance to be heard when major business issues are being discussed. And there's an obligation on the CIO, as well, to stay intimately aware of the strategies driving the business, so that IT's efforts can be supportive of the goals of the company and sensitive to the priorities of the individual business units. This is a topic we'll return to on several occasions in these pages.

How these arrangements stand at different companies, and how the present arrangements were arrived at, holds some surprises. Kregg Jodie commented that at Mary Kay, "Six or seven years ago, the CIO wasn't part of the staff meetings led by the Chief Operating Officer or the President. The information was being fed to somebody who had IT responsibility under his wing, but who didn't have much technology experience. Strategic plans were not being laid out in a cohesive fashion throughout the company. Today," Kregg said, "the senior executives meet for two hours a week developing strategic plans and communications." He is a participant, and even coordinates the agenda.

Aligning the IT plans with the strategic business plan is much easier, since Kregg is not just familiar with the business strategy but helped create it. How does a change like that come about? Kregg explained that their status began to improve as an outcome of the website project—

> The success with our e-business undertakings enhanced the credibility of the IT department. We also strengthened the business focus of IT and developed the organization, which made it more strategic in terms of delivering measurable results.
>
> The people at the executive level at that time were open-minded toward considering IT more strategically, and are to be commended for embracing technology.
>
> When I took over as CIO, we made it our focus to show the value that technology could provide for Mary Kay. And then once we had credibility with the executives, it was much easier to partner with the various business functions to initiate and implement ideas enabled with technology. President and COO David Holl made sure that we moved IT leadership from the programming room to the board room.

We've talked for years and years about insuring that IT is integrated into the business planning process, but how well is that happening today? As Bill Simon and I said in our last book, if you're a senior business leader today and you're not at least basically literate technically, then you're unqualified to fill your position.

I still find examples of CEOs and other C-level officers who refuse to have anything to do with technology. Of course, expecting executives to be technologically literate doesn't mean turning them into programmers. But it does mean expecting them to use the Internet regularly, use email on their own, know how to move through an electronic spreadsheet, and even know how to modify it. Because corporate leaders who don't have some comfort level with technology tend to be the same ones who haven't yet figured out that their technology chief ought to be a member of the top management team.

Residential Capital Group of GMAC-RFC, under Rick Greenwood's IT leadership, has seen that transition of status take place. When he took on his present job, he was not "sitting at the table" as part of the group's senior leadership team. As he puts it, "I was sitting in the row *behind* the senior management table."

> You know, as our group president might say, you have to earn the right to sit at that table. So that was our goal from the first—to earn that right. It depends on your ability to do what you say you're going to execute on, and then show the value that you're bringing. So for the first year, I was CIO reporting to the group president. He had a team of what he believed to be his key managers, and IT was in a kind of advisory role to those key managers.
>
> Over time, I think he saw that technology was a main driver. It was a main force for him to be able to create better value for our business partners and for the homeowners, our ultimate customers. My IT team was able to demonstrate not just our ability to execute, but our ability to understand the business.
>
> This is a point of distinction and a value we bring—how to apply the solutions to solve their business problems or their need of enabling some capability. We showed we could listen to a problem and explain in business terms how IT could provide a solution.
>
> Then our president went through a revamping of the organization in which he established a portfolio of six interdependent business units within the Residential Capital Group. And

within that reorganization, he also decided to have key services to be at the table. He decided that IT should be part of that group of key managers.

So I became an equal partner with the others in the key strategic planning process.

If you're not sitting at the table when the team is doing the strategic planning or business planning and so forth, you're definitely going to be on the short end of the stick.

Rick admits that the process is not yet "well oiled and going well." On the plus side of the ledger, "There is very effective dialog, very effective exchange of information." He says—

When an initiative comes up, there is key strategic planning to understand in depth what the impact of that initiative is and what it would lead to. And we're involved in that process.

If you're not sitting at the table when the team is doing the strategic planning or business planning and so forth, you're definitely going to be on the short end of the stick.

The requirement for earning this coveted spot on the senior management team, Rick says, is that "You have to have some kind of intimate business knowledge, so you can help enhance the vision they're trying to create. And that's the part that my group CEO keeps challenging me on: 'Bring value to our portfolio of businesses.'"

For some time now, the better technology leaders have been hungry for their top management to make more of an effort toward understanding the business reasons for technology expenditures,. And, as well, for reaching the point of having their own philosophy about the contribution of technology to the business. Roger Smith—

The responsibility needs to be shouldered by IT, as well, by helping management understand that our technical knowledge allows us to add to the success of the business and allows us to help them solve challenges and problems.

One major-company CIO put this in an especially colorful way: "We can't just be order takers. IT isn't a waitress saying, 'Do you want it rare or well done?' If we listen and understand what their challenges are, we should be able to be creative enough to say, 'Well, if that's the problem, then we could use this kind of technology, and it should able to go a certain distance to answering that need.'"

Technology and the Corporate Leaders

At Washington Mutual, the role of CIO is moving a step beyond as the current holder of that job, Jerry Gross, takes on a higher level of responsibility—

> We're in the process of looking for a Chief Technology Officer, who would pick up more of the technical aspects of the job. I'll remain CIO, but take on broader responsibilities. I'm spending more of my time thinking about new business models for the company and how we can use technology to get to know our customers better, and how we can be proactive in serving and cross-selling our customers. A lot of my role now is going to be involved in that direction.

In fact, Jerry sees this as a natural evolution of what a CIO should be—

> It gets back to those three buckets—you know, run the business, grow the business, and innovate the business. First you get the basic infrastructure in place and get the business running cost effectively. If you don't get that going, there's no way to get to the next bucket.
>
> Once you've got all those things, you can start to get the governance pieces tied down on growing the business. And then it's about evolution of the business R&D. We're spending a lot of time right now on building a business plan for an innovation center for Washington Mutual—not just a technology innovation center, but a business innovation center where we could pilot and innovate products and services with our business partners, and then launch those for our customers.

Lloyds TSB bank is one of the largest financial institutions in England. At the time we spoke with him for this book, Archie Kane was responsible for the bank's technologies and a member of the bank's senior board of directors. He had recently moved to take on new responsibilities, as well: the Chairman asked him to take over the task of heading a business unit, an outfit recently acquired by Lloyds. So Archie is now president of a major business, an insurance company with a name that to Americans sounds like a joke: Scottish Widows. Nonetheless, Archie is a textbook case of someone coming up from the technology side, who manages to understand the business issues so well that he eventually takes on an operational role.

From his perspective as the technology boss for five years, Archie has been in good position to observe changes in the relationships between the business side of Lloyds and the technology side. His disappointment in relation to improvements in this relationship seemed surprising—

> If I'm honest about it, I'm less satisfied than I thought I would be at this stage. Things have improved, but they've not improved as quickly as I hoped and planned that they would. I still see a significant gulf between the business leaders and the technology issues. It's not as bad as it was, but it's not as good as it should be.
>
> This is one of the key issues we're focusing on. We have this program in place called 'Improving IT.' We have an IT person sitting as part of all of the executive teams in the various business areas. In the past, some of the business units have done this, and some haven't; now, all of them do. We've taken a much stronger stance: You've got to have an IT guy as part of your business executive team.
>
> The IT representative is there to listen, all day, every day, to any problems. 'Your problems are his problems.' We didn't push that as hard in the past as we're now. So I think that's part of the fix.
>
> And I think we need to convince business leaders that when they come out with a good strategy but discover they can't execute on it, technology may be one of the reasons.

That's asking IT to be a partner in solving a problem once the damage is done. How about making IT a partner in designing the project from the outset? That's part of the message that the better technology leaders are trying to convey.

Archie Kane adds on this subject—

> The only good strategies are the ones that you can actually execute. There aren't any other good strategies. And technology is sometimes a reason why it's difficult to execute, but my honest feeling is that it's usually not the primary reason. The primary reason is the ability of a business to handle change. Technology often used to be the major limiting factor, but I don't see that being true any longer.

In Archie's view, technology could be delivering a good deal more value to the business units; it's the business side that isn't yet ready to handle the change.

In a perfect world, the head of any major IT organization would always be a person who could also run a business. That doesn't mean I believe that all IT people need to have this as their goal, but any IT leader who deserves a seat at the table certainly needs to have a greater understanding of the business than most business managers will ever have of IT.

The Small-Company Experience

Maybe it's not immediately obvious, but smaller companies sometimes have lessons to teach the managers and leaders of larger firms about handling technology matters. In a small company, the CEO is so much closer to IT that he's highly likely to have a much more intimate knowledge of the technology issues. The potential gain from good decisions, and the potential impact from bad ones, can be drastic.

David Wilson is the founder and President of East Industries, a small company in Rocky Mount, North Carolina. The company is part of a $7 billion industry that most people would never have dreamed existed. After burning out on his first post-college job in the textiles industry, David noticed that the nearby plant of a national pharmaceutical company was using a large number of wooden pallets. Off in a corner of their yard sat a lonely pile of wreckage, the ugly remains of what had once been serviceable pallets. David tracked down the right person to talk to and found the company would be happy to have someone turn the wreckage into something other than a total loss. From that conversation, East Industries was born.

At that time, most shipping managers figured that any pallet damaged in shipment belonged on the scrap heap. David started removing and sometimes buying the scrap, restoring the pallets to usable condition, and selling them back—often to the same company he had bought the scrap from. He's now been at it for twenty years, along with other companies he has started and still runs.

David has a strong commitment to seeing that his managers work as a team—

> I can tell you one thing about pulling a culture together. We have a staff meeting just about every Wednesday at 9:00. We hook up a tablet PC to a docking station, drop down the big 8 by 8 screen out of the ceiling and crank up the projector.
>
> Then we go through issues that have come up. Everybody's got a department that they're controlling—production, main-

tenance, facilities, equipment, and so on. We open up their department on the task management system and he goes through what he said last time that he wanted to accomplish during the week, and how they did, and any problems they encountered. And then he tells everybody what areas need to be addressed for the coming week and what his goals are. These tasks and objectives are then typed in and show up on the viewing screen.

And everybody kind of pulls together because they just gained an appreciation of what the other person is doing.

At the end of the meeting, we've already got all the tasks printed out for each participant. They get a copy as they walk out the door, and that's their task list for the next week.

You know how a lot of meetings go: you sit there and everybody takes different notes, and afterward it's 'That's not what I thought you said.' But this way we do it on the screen, live, real time, and when they leave they've got a hardcopy. They might not get all the items done, but it brings the culture together. Everybody gets a feeling for what the others are doing, that the others all do have problems, too. It makes for a very cohesive culture. We're building some sense of community rather than everyone isolated on their own island.

To me, that's a classic example of using technology to enhance what might be called the emotional aspects of management.

Before, we'd have short meetings, I'd sit down and talk with one department; they'd raise some issues and we'd make some decisions, and they'd go away and take care of it. And it was mostly verbal—there wasn't any record of, 'What was the problem? What was the decision?'

I saw a big change once these meetings started. Everybody felt the camaraderie of us all working together as a team. This way everybody's on the same page. It's just a great process. We've had it going on for three years now, and as simple as it is, it's a very cohesive force. Everybody knows from one week to the next where we are, where we've been doing things, why things didn't work, cost overruns, or we made things look pretty and whatever it was.

I think it's just a good way of managing a small business.

That's top-down support at work.

David gives much credit to his outside technology consultant, Jason Harrison of Harrison Technologies, who he credits with being "a very good long-term thinker." The important issue: "He understands the big picture and he understands our business."

> I'm privileged to have somebody who can have enough insight to see what emerging technology we need to manage our business.

Take-Aways

In this chapter, our respondents raised two aspects of the leadership issue: leadership of the CEO on technology issues, and leadership of the company's technology chief.

With respect to the CIO, in today's climate he or she needs to be a person with a strong grasp of business issues, and needs to have ability to demonstrate the possibilities for IT: the potential contributions of how technology can help solve business problems.

A third issue involves the essential need for a strong connection between IT planning and business planning—a subject we'll be addressing in some depth in a later chapter.

A final topic raised in this chapter was the issue of education. The superstar CIOs are those who take it upon themselves to educate their peers about technology.

In addition, the CIO needs to take a leadership role in integrating the planning process for technology, with the business planning process of the enterprise.

The interviews for this chapter provided a list of imperatives for the CEO—starting with a willingness to becoming open to learning about technology. And one of the things every CEO should be learning is that his Chief Information Officer can be a valuable contributor when issues of corporate strategy are being discussed. He or she should—in the phrase used here—have a seat at the table.

Finally, the CEO should, as well, be his company's prime driver for change management—controlling the resources that must be engaged for change, and personally taking the reins of change management.

2

Anybody Buying Technology Only for the Sake of the Technology Just Doesn't Get It

> It's not about the technology, it's about what's between the ears of individuals and their willingness to change and use the technology.
>
> —Dave Clementz, *CIO, ChevronTexaco*

Since the dot-com bubble burst, my company and a great many others—probably including yours—have grown a great deal fussier and more particular about how money gets spent. The caution is certainly appropriate but, in terms of technology, calls for a mindset that many companies have been missing.

What is the value of providing a particular tool set for the sales force to be more productive? What is the value associated with providing technologies that allow people to conduct meetings remotely rather than having to come together? What is the value associated with investing heavily in technology that allows you to get your products to market more quickly?

Everyone agrees your company needs an accounting system. It's much harder to get agreement that the sales-force tool or the remote-meeting software will bring some bottom-line benefit. To answer questions like these, business leadership has to be hard on themselves in figuring out if the benefits can actually be achieved.

We'll explore the challenge from three different perspectives.

USING TECHNOLOGY FOR COMPETITIVE ADVANTAGE

Soaring with JetBlue

JetBlue Airways was formed in March 2000, probably the worst year ever for launching a start-up in the airline industry. Yet the company has had a string of profitable quarters that would be impressive in any industry—but is especially striking for an airline. From a corporate culture perspective, founder and CEO David Neeleman began with the idea of offering the consumer an alternative to the travel experience on the larger airlines in terms of quality of service, on-time arrival, and all of the other measures that frequent fliers gauge an airline against. In fact, he likes to describe JetBlue not as an airline but as a services company.

This wasn't the first time around for Neeleman. He had started another airline, Morris Air, several years earlier. When that company was bought by Southwest Airlines, the capital investment firm that had financed the venture reportedly turned their $14 million stake into $42 million in one year. As part of the deal, Neeleman became a Southwest executive. The arrangement, however, was short-lived: "After five or six months, they were as sick of me as I was of them," he told a reporter for Forbes.

When it came time to start JetBlue, Neeleman said, "I raised the money—$130 million—in two weeks. We had no gates, no planes, nothing. But the investors know me and trust me. Plus, I'm a good storyteller."

He proved to be more than a good storyteller. Besides the applaudable decision to emphasize service, he made some excellent decisions about technology. In building their infrastructure, his idea was to think about how to reduce expenses below what's typical in the industry, such as their reservation system. As described in the Introduction to this book (see p. *xi*), the system was built just as any other airline would build it, and was linked with other established airlines, yet is vastly less expensive to operate because there is no massive call center.

One of the things that most determines the success or failure of an airline is how much time its airplanes spend in the air. And one of the impediments to that process is the enormous paperwork burden on aircraft maintenance personnel—all part of making sure the planes are properly maintained and safe to fly, but a huge burden nonetheless.

JetBlue's answer: the airline built a system that allows the mechanics to do all of their reporting online. That led to a significant decrease in the number of errors, which had been an unavoidable part of the paperwork approach. As a result, JetBlue planes spend more time in the air flying than the average for the industry.

And similarly for the pilots. The FAA requires pilots to update their flight manuals whenever a change is issued for the aircraft they fly, and for the air traffic control procedures they're required to follow; the flurry of changes can number several a week. (The documentation is so voluminous that one old airman's tongue-in-cheek adages says that "The airplane is ready to fly when the weight of the paperwork equals the weight of the aircraft.") Airline pilots find the process of keeping their manuals updated—tearing out the old sheets and replacing with the new—a necessary nuisance. But not at JetBlue. The company issues every pilot a laptop computer, and each morning their manuals are automatically updated over the company's Intranet site.

Even so, as pointed out earlier, JetBlue budgets 1.4 percent of total revenues on information technology in an industry where the standard is 5 percent. And from a serving-your-customer perspective, *Condé Nast Traveler* magazine ranks the airline tops in customer satisfaction. So here's a company running at the peak of its game from the customer satisfaction and profit measurements, and its percentage expenditure on technology is running vastly less than the rest of its industry.

Delivering Customer Benefit: A Trial Project That Worked Out

I'm always intrigued when I find a company that sees a piece of new technology and wonders, "Can we use that? Would it improve our processes in some way? Would it give us a competitive advantage?" So the following story was a pleasure to hear and is a pleasure to share.

The speaker is Rachelle Mileur, who at the time was Director of eCommerce Systems Development at Airborne, the package delivery company since acquired by DHL.

A team of IT people had learned about a new product from a major software firm that I won't name because it would sound like an advertisement. They decided to try one small project to see if the new application could provide a quick solution as promised. Here's Rachelle's story of how the experience unfolded—

> We were trying to come up with ways that we could evaluate the product and deliver business value at the same time. The IT goal was to test drive the software and see if it provided as much productivity as touted. And from a business perspective, you can't do that unless you deliver immediate value.

The single most important question people ask a package delivery firm is, "Where's my package?" The Airborne team wanted to see if they could find a way to improve how they provided this information to customers, and, hopefully, in the process, gain a competitive advantage—

> If we could push that information out to customers, if we could make the information readily available on their desktops, then we could save them a phone call, and perhaps cut down on the phone traffic to our call centers.

The process of getting this effort off the ground began with piquing the interest of the business side. They wanted to try to leverage the company's existing database as an interface to obtaining tracking information—

> One benefit that this solution had was that it would only require about ten weeks of development, in addition to having a very low cost of entry from a software purchase point of view. So the hurdle to get over in terms of proving business benefits was lower.

That brought the effort to a juncture of special interest in this book—an issue we'll come back to over and over: the relationship between a company's technology group and its business units. At Airborne, IT clearly had already established a good working relationship with the business units, and the two partnered on developing the financials and obtaining a budget for the project.

The new service gives Airborne an important competitive advantage over FedEx, which charges customers for a similar service that allows viewing of all shipments and their status—

Our offering was based on saying that most often the customer doesn't want to know about all fifty packages he's shipped, but rather about one in particular. So he wants to pick that one and be told when it arrived. We provide that service to our customers for free.

If it's en route, he'll see an update every time the package reaches another place where it's scanned by a driver, or at an Airborne facility.

For Airborne, this wasn't just an innovative project—it was the opening of a door on a new paradigm, a new approach for delivering business improvements—

Traditionally, projects have been delivered a system at a time; they're groupings of functionality. In a weak economy, it's a sign of the times that a business is less willing to risk a large amount of capital in hopes that the projected benefits of a large-scale project will really be achieved. Instead, we're trying to work with a business that asks for less cost by asking them to just tell us the essence of what they need and let us deliver that, and then over time we can add to it.

If you will, it's the house analogy. Instead of delivering you an entirely finished home including the drapes and curtains, ready to move in, I want to start by giving you a structure that's secure—it has walls and a roof, the basic plumbing, windows, and a front door you can lock, but it doesn't have much beyond that. It certainly doesn't have any of the fine touches. And then, over time, I will add to it.

A large wireless carrier we're working with is looking to roll the solution out to all of their sales desktops. If they have a customer who needs a replacement phone—let's say you're like me and your life depends on your integrated pocket PC, cell phone, and coffee maker—when it breaks, then you better get the replacement to that customer quick or they'll find a carrier who will.

In those sort of high-value shipping opportunities, the tracking of a package is really important, and it allows the sales force to be involved by letting the sales person know when a package has arrived. A service like this could actually be the reason that a customer chooses us, because it makes their sales force more productive and makes their customers happier.

The challenge in the shipping business is not so much getting a package there on time, but rather being able to assist a customer in finding out where that package is and when it will be there if it isn't going to arrive on time. The customer is less likely to be mad if you tell them before the package is supposed to arrive that it's been delayed. This solution gives us a chance to allow our customers, or the customers of our customers, to be better informed.

Sometimes even a small technology solution can yield a significant advantage.

Competitive Advantage for the Smaller Company

Can a smaller company find competitive advantage in technology?

Based in Bellevue, Washington, Telesystems West sells and installs phone systems to small and midsize companies in the Puget Sound area. Founder Terry Szpak (it's pronounced "Spak") could be a poster boy for the American dream. In 1991, his career working as a technician for major telecommunications companies came to an abrupt halt when he was laid off. He had the new house, the new baby, and no job. Just before Christmas.

Instead of applying for unemployment, he launched a business in his basement. "I was sort of forced into it," he said. "I went from there and I've never looked back. About six months later, I got a call to return to that company." Terry and his partner weren't making much money at that point, but, "I just decided, 'I'm not gonna go back and have that next layoff hanging over my head.'"

Today Telesystems boasts annual revenues approaching $2 million and serves a client base of five thousand customers. But not long ago, Terry recognized a growing problem of continuing glitches in coordinating the schedules of their ten field technicians, who were being dispatched in a process that involved endless phone calls and an ongoing flurry of e-mails. Meanwhile, the records for billable time and parts used flooded the office in an avalanche of scraps of paper and handwritten notes.

Terry explained, "We have technicians from Camano Island in the north to Auburn in the south. And if you're familiar enough with the Seattle area to know those places, you also know the traffic situation here." To alleviate the situation, Telesystems put their own technology to work. He gave each of their field reps a choice: continue coming into the office every morning to pick up your assignments, and returning at the end of the day to turn in your time sheets. Or let the company install a computer in your home, a high-speed Internet connection, and Voice over IP. "It's part of one of the systems we sell. It enables employees to work from home in what amounts to a call-center environment."

No surprise: every one chose to communicate from home. "So now when we dispatch people, we can keep them out of the traffic as much as possible, and we can determine who goes to which customers more efficiently."

According to Szpak, the new system has saved the company up to an hour a day for each technician—hours that are being used not on the freeway, but as billable time. "It also saves us office space, and we only need about half as many parking spots. And the guys are happy with it because they can go directly home after their work is done."

The difference shows up on the company's bottom line as a revenue increase of $100,000 a year. Each evening, the technicians sit at their home computers and enter in the billable time and parts information, which goes directly into a corporate database—resulting in an estimated 5 to 10 percent gain in accuracy.

Beating the Competition in an Off-Beat Industry

Earlier we met David Wilson, founder of a company in the little-encountered business of manufacturing and refurbishing shipping pallets. The company flourished, but in the last five years the competitive situation began to change.

"A lot of the smaller companies have faded out, and lately there's been a very strong movement for companies to merge," David explained. That changed the face of the industry. "You now have stronger and larger players that can stretch their tentacles out into more diverse geographic areas because of the nature of their capitalization and services offered, and they can go in and service large accounts that have multiple locations. This was unheard of prior to five years ago."

How does a small company survive in a climate like this? David explains:

Pricing has a lot to do with it, but so does loyalty based on service. In this business we're like shrimp boats going out and gleaning a harvest. We have to go to companies that we don't sell to that generate these surplus pallets, and competitively bid to get them in here so we can reutilize them.

One reason we have invested in the technology is to sustain our position as best as possible. As things change and evolve, we're trying to stay a little bit ahead of the curve on the technology side because other areas are relatively set: labor costs are pretty much the same for everybody, and there haven't been any advances in the mechanized systems to handle the materials. So technology has been the one edge. We've really invested time and money into it, to give our customers something our competition is not giving.

This has completely changed the competitive climate for companies like East Industries. David has to be able to compete on something other than price—

You really have to be able to say, 'Okay, yes, you can go do business with those other people, but here are the benefits that they can't offer you.'

We've done this with several accounts simply through technology because we have such good accounting systems, which we started building about ten years ago, and it's really helped us maintain our customer base. It lets us give the customer instant information of their status with us.

We've recently set up a real-time accounting database where the customers come into our website and see the accounting details of where they stand with us.

A few have talked about taking their business away, going elsewhere. It's never really been about service, but it's usually cost issues. Or they might have problems and say, 'Hey, we're just way out of kilter on our budget.' And we say, 'Here's where we are, here's what's happening, what can we tweak this way or the other to get you back in your budget realm? What do we need to do?' That just wouldn't be possible if we didn't really have good accounting data.

Without that, I think some of our best customers would have gone elsewhere. But since we do such a good job of it, the local managers within a fifty or seventy-five mile radius have mostly stayed with us.

Does 'Competitive Advantage' Have Meaning When Profit's Not the Motive?

Most people would say that the phrase 'competitive advantage' doesn't translate into the world of non-profits and governmental agencies. But hold your hat; the Army's Carla von Bernewitz offered this observation—

> If you change the question to *strategic* advantage, then the answer is most definitely 'yes.' We definitely understand strategic advantage. For us it's not, 'Are we going beat out a competitor?' Rather, the strategic advantage is being able to do our job better than the next guy. In our case, that means winning the next war.
>
> And I think we finally have come to the realization that it's not just the visible tools that give us advantage. We're now tying together those non-warfighting systems—the back-office business computers and networks and so on—with the warfighting systems. It was the realization that we weren't going to have a strategic advantage if we couldn't tie them together.

Does this reasoning apply to non-profits and governmental agencies? Sure: for "non-fighting," read "IT staff"; for "fighting," read "the business side"—which brings us right back to a main theme of this book, getting IT and the business units working closely enough to understand each other.

USING TECHNOLOGY FOR REDUCING COSTS

Many companies seem to overlook ways that technology might aid in reducing operating costs. Here are a few that set an example.

We heard in the previous chapter from Craig Cuyar, the CIO of CommonHealth. Craig has responsibility for providing worldwide IT infrastructure support services, business development services, and more, across all of the company's sixteen subsidiaries. CommonHealth numbers several of the major pharmaceutical companies among their important clients, and Craig described how a little homework revealed a way the company could save money for these clients and create a new source of revenue for itself:

> We spoke to a number of our clients and found out that they are under increased scrutiny for their costs—just like everybody

else with a downturn in the economy. One of the areas that came back to us—that all of these clients were looking to eliminate—were the costs associated with the movement of files, their digital assets, between and among our companies, our clients, and our client's vendors such as printers and CD-ROM duplication facilities.

Because of stringent requirements of the Food and Drug Administration, an ad in the healthcare field needs to undergo multiple legal, medical, and regulatory reviews from the client pharmaceutical company before it appears in print. But these steps are always last minute, on a very tight timeline, and every day that CommonHealth can bring a campaign to market earlier than expected translates into increased revenue for the client—

> The traditional method is that when the job is done, ready to go out the door to the vendor, we put the file onto a CD or DVD, drop it into a FedEx envelope, and they get it about 11 o'clock the next morning. We quickly realized that if we could compress that time element so that they have instantaneous access to the file, we could speed up the process and at the same time get rid of the delivery charges.
>
> We did a quick analysis for one of our clients and found that they spent $112,000 in out-of-pocket fees for courier costs in 2002. So we built a system as a document repository. When we have a file ready for release, instead of putting it on a CD and dropping it in the FedEx envelope, we now publish it to this document repository, and an alert e-mail is automatically generated to the client informing them that the file has been released. They then have a twofold benefit: instant access to the file and no out-of-pocket costs for the courier services .
>
> In this specific example, the client that was spending $112,000 a year, I was able to sell the system to them for $50,000. They're happy at lowering their costs; I'm happy that we've put a system in place that generates revenue for an IT organization.

That's a clear case of using technology to lower a client's costs. The same principle works as well at much smaller companies, as was made clear by East Industries' David Wilson:

> We have to manage this business on a per-piece arrangement—90 percent of our employees in the production areas

are on a per-piece scale. They get so much every time they cut a board, so much every time they handle a pallet, and so on. So we have a tremendous number of items to keep the beans counted correctly. But it's essential both from a payment standpoint, and also from a management standpoint, to keep track of the materials that are recovered for rework or remanufacture for a particular customer, and so on.

We couldn't have kept control of this business the way we run it if we hadn't been smart about technology starting a long time ago. And then to put all that data together so you kind of know where you stand, and base it against your annual budgets and make sure that you're within your budgets. And find out what areas you're weakest in and strongest in.

One reason we've invested in the technology is to sustain our position as best as possible. We're trying to stay a little bit ahead of the curve on the technology side because other areas don't give us much chance to compete. Technology does.

From the other side, we can keep up with the realities of what it's costing us to operate almost on a daily basis. Now that we have this [technology], I think it's absolutely critical to have the availability of that information. Yes, you'll spot a trend even without this, but sometimes things can go south in a hurry when you're moving thousands of batches through the system. You can't wait till the end of the month to find out. You've gotta figure a quick response and jump on it right away.

In some smaller businesses, when the times are booming as in the nineties, you can get away with a little looser oversight of the detail. But when the climate gets tight, it becomes even more important because one swing the wrong way can drive a small business from happiness to unhappiness overnight.

David's answer to what makes him so sure that technology has made a difference—

Number one, number two, and number three: We're still in business. That's always a good thing. And we're poised to take advantage of the next wave of pallet development—re-manufactured pallets. That's becoming the next big niche in the pallet market. I just know that the level of confidence we've been able to establish by providing our customers with the data that they need when they need it is making a crucial difference.

As another area of improvement, East Industries beefed up its pallet inventory management system to capture vital data. Now David and his executives are able to access and use information more effectively to better manage employee productivity and improve customer service and communication. The overall impact of the solution is expected to yield a cost savings of 10 to 15 percent.

For me, this company in many ways represents a classic example of what you'd like to see as the 'business' approach to technology. What drives their interest is not the technology in itself, it's the company's business priorities. Because as much of a technology enthusiast as David might be, you can go too far the other way. As he made clear, he's aware of that danger.

Here was the CEO of a relatively small company, both knowledgeable about and focused on the opportunity for technology to have this kind of significant impact in his business. Most of the small companies that have traditionally been his competitors, David Wilson said, are beginning to use technology more than they used to. Even in the palette refurbishing industry, technology is taking hold!

At another small firm, based in Las Vegas, owner Karen Settle told us, "Technology is the main core of how we run the business, how we communicate with our field people, and how we keep our customers happy." Her company, Keystone Marketing Services, has two hundred field people who visit retail electronics and computer stores on behalf of technology vendors. The reps train the local sales people, and work with store management to set up displays featuring their client companies' products. In operation for ten years, the business grosses about $5 million annually.

Karen is typical of the small-business owner who recognizes the need to keep tabs on how the company could be using technology better—

Originally when field reps did a call, they would fill out a call visit form and fax it in to us. I had a staff of data input people entering the data into a spreadsheet. And then as we grew, we had a programmer build us a customized program. I told the programmer, 'We don't want to input anymore, we want to be out of the input business.'

With that first version of customized software, the field people were e-mailing their reports in. We kept one person who did report analysis and monthly reports for our clients.

And then as the Internet evolved we said, 'This is crazy, let's use the Internet.' For the next version of the reporting system, I wanted us to be able to have the software analyze the data instead of keeping a staff person who sits there and just does reports. And that person's salary helped us afford the new version of the software. The break-even was about two years.

According to Karen, being able to recover the cost of the new software quickly was only one small part of the incentive. The additional convenience to clients helped the company grow faster. And there may be an additional payoff, beside—

I've looked at taking that system and leasing it to other companies because it's such a powerful system. It pulls together our scheduling and our reporting and our payroll, and that really does run the business—everything is communicated to the field from there.

We're going to be adding the capability for the field people to go into a store and take digital pictures, and upload them along with their report. A client going into the file will look at the pictures and see how his products are being displayed on the retail sales floor.

So we're looking at how do we grow it and how do we expand. And it's all basically Internet based.

USING TECHNOLOGY FOR IMPROVING PRODUCTIVITY

Doctors, Nurses, and Productivity

Integris Health, the largest not-for-profit healthcare organization in the state of Oklahoma, records $1.1 billion in annual revenues. CIO Avery Cloud was brought in four years ago to chase the e-business vision and create a technology road map for improving productivity and increasing profitability. One of his avowed goals: "We intend to make this organization paperless, for both financials and clinical records, by 2006."

Here's a CIO who insists that the value of IT doesn't lie primarily in replacing employees. "That's a misplaced financial model," he says. "If I'm told the value of the system is to replace an employ-ee, I'll disagree." In his view, if an IT system improves productivity for the nursing staff, he believes the time saved ought to be rein-vested in something else, like "spending time with doctors and making sure that patient care is documented properly. Because this equates to reimbursement to us that can add a lot to the bot-tom line."

He's proud that "we haven't laid anyone off, but we've improved the financial position of this company." And he points out, "I know hospitals with over 300 employees. I think we're doing a better job with less than 200. It's about working smarter, not harder." Healthcare isn't a bastion of e-business expertise; in Avery's view, "As an industry, we're ten years behind in applying IT to business problems."

But the situation is different at Integris. "Our CEO is a visionary," says Cloud.

The CEO he puts on a pedestal is Stan Hupfeld, who has been with the predecessor organization since the 1980s, when he was run-ning a hospital in Texas. Stan tells the story of his hiring this way: "I got a call from a recruiter who asked me if I was interested in apply-ing for the job of President of Baptist Medical Center in Oklahoma City. He described the job and I told him it sounded really interest-ing but he needed to understand two things. I said, 'First, I'm Catholic, and secondly, I went to the University of Texas.' And there was a long pause and he said, 'You know, I think we can handle the Catholic part.'"

(In fact, Stan didn't just go to the University of Texas; he played on the 1963 national champion football team—although, he insists, "not very well.")

Stan's connection with health care started in the military, serv-ing in Vietnam as a Surgeon's Assistant. The work grabbed his interest and, except for time spent getting a master's degree, he's been in the field ever since—long enough that he can say, "I'm old enough to remember when people wrote the charges that doctors made on a piece of paper and put it in a vacuum tube and sent it somewhere."

Still, as most everybody who has been inside a hospital recog-nizes, there's a long way to go. People on the inside of the industry understand that even better than the rest of us, as Stan Hupfeld made clear:

If you would follow an average nurse around, what you would find in most hospitals is that she spends 40 percent of her time writing. Every time they do something to or for the patient, they make a note of it. They might make a note on a piece of paper or they might make a note on their hand. And then they go transcribe that note into the official record.

And then, to that, add the amount of time physicians spend dealing with records.

If we could only automate this process. For instance, I've always had this vision of a nurse with a little lapel mike going from patient to patient, dictating as she went, and that would automatically be put in the patient's record and it would be totally hands free and totally paperless. And I think we'll get there at some point in time.

But certainly, from the perspective of the administration of our employees, there's an enormous efficiency to be gained once the technology reaches the point that it's easier than writing it down.

There have been some attempts at automating this process, but so far the right answer hasn't been found—

We've seen some spectacular failures in our industry over the last couple of years, where hospitals or health systems said that on February 1, everybody is going to do their notes on the computer and we're not going to have any handwritten notes anymore. And for the most part, physicians were either unwilling or unable to comply, and there was a major breakdown, and people had to return to the old system.

Part of the problem now under almost any scenario is that it's still quicker for a physician to tell somebody, or yell at the nurse, or write it down themselves, than it is to log onto a computer and go through those series of menus. And so under that best of circumstances with current technology, you're gonna add on the front end of the physician's workload. And that is clearly unacceptable for a busy doctor.

There is an argument, of course, that if you interface with the computer and do all your work through the computer that you save on the back end, in terms of clarification and 'I can't read your writing, doctor.' I think it can be done, but it's just going to have to be a lot faster than it is now. Maybe voice recognition will do that.

Meanwhile, the new federal legislation on patient privacy certainly has made it more difficult—signing on is more difficult, and the requirements for changing passwords, and so on, have complicated the technology solution.

With the shortage of nurses today, and with ever-rising healthcare costs a problem for almost every family and every business, certainly the hospital industry is a place where improvements in productivity would be most welcome. But not at the expense of quality; all of us want the best care we can get, at an affordable cost. It's a role made to order for technology.

Productivity Push

In 2002, the management of ChevronTexaco decided that its recent investment in a digital infrastructure should be able to yield a doubling in productivity. The task of making that happen was handed to David Clementz, president of ChevronTexaco Information Technology Company. David started the drive by coming up with a catchy label: the "Productivity Push"—

> What we're going to do—and we're well on our way to achieving it this year [2003]—is that we're going to boost the productivity of the firm by 10 percent. We talk to each unit and ask them to figure out how they're doing things now, and can they do 10 percent more. Can they do 10 percent faster?
>
> When my boss said he wanted to double the productivity, I said, 'Well, that's fine, we'll use the doubling rule. I'll give it to you in seven years—10 percent a year for seven years, and we'll be doubled.' Because it's not about the technology, it's about what's between the ears of individuals and their willingness to change and use the technology.

Dave's path to becoming CIO was, to say the least, unusual. He holds a doctorate in, of all things, a field called "soil science." It turns out that's not as weird as it at first sounds: figuring out how to extract oil from underground deposits has a lot to do with understanding the physics and chemistry of the soil.

Then it came out in the conversation that Dave doesn't have a background in information technology. The CIO of a $100 billion company doesn't have a technology background?! He explained that he had been the company's chief engineer in Canada for a time, and was later sent to the company's research and development organization—

> I had been sent there to reorganize, and we struggled with the business model to try to really understand what it cost to deliver a single product or service. I solved that by creating a model based on activity-based cost accounting.

His success wasn't going unnoticed—

> Within two years, I became president of the R&D organization. After another two years, the Chairman called me in and said he wanted me to install the same business model within IT. And he wanted me to do it as the CIO.
>
> Although I had been a power user of information systems, the bits and bytes were a mystery to me. My first response was 'No.' But I figured it was going to be career-limiting if I didn't accept. The organization has a lot of competent, really strong technical people. So I took the job and stayed focused on the business; my predecessor had been more focused on the technology.

The Productivity Push effort has reached out to every level of the company—

> This is the sort of thing you can't drive from the top. What you can drive from the top is the knowledge of what's there. And that's what the Productivity Push was all about. We were going to train everybody in the tools on their desktop. My guru, Joe Stanko, set up a band of disciples who went forth into the operating company and are doing the training out there, looking at their business processes. They teach how to do spreadsheets out in the field so that people can take their operational data and stream it right into these databases, and see things that they never saw before.

Here he was touching on an idea that I think is critical. In my experience working with hundreds of companies, few of them have as part of their culture the commitment to empowering people through training in the technology that the company has bought, paid for, and put onto dozens, hundreds, or thousands of employees' computers. When people learn how to use the technology they already have, they not only become more productive but start discovering innovative, highly valuable ways to use it. Sometimes all it takes is just getting your people started. Clementz agreed: "When you get individuals empowered with the tools that are on their desktop, things change." He continued—

> We're teaching everybody how to use Outlook, how to use NetMeeting and its successors, how to use Instant Messaging. These tools for a global company are so powerful that we're already seeing groups changing the way they do their work. We have people just pop on Instant Messaging now instead of making phone calls. In our South America operations especially, we're seeing Instant Messaging used big time.
>
> And all of a sudden, people are finding new ways to work together using the spreadsheet program. If we have accountants in this firm who don't know how to use the spreadsheet program, then shame on them.
>
> Even for me, I had my productivity guru come and sit with me for one hour and show me how to use my e-mail program more effectively. I used to take about three hours a day to do e-mail. He showed me how to set up rules, I made messages go in certain folders, I made messages disappear that I didn't want to see. I color-coded my incoming messages—the Chairman's messages now arrive in bright red. Now it takes me about an hour to do all my e-mail. So I boosted my own personal productivity on e-mail by a factor of three—actually three orders of magnitude.

When Dave found out that one of the senior executives had some thousand e-mails in his Inbox, he decided it was time to figure out a way of getting some training for the top management team. Not easy for people who have a tall stack of high-priority items waiting for their attention. He came up with what I consider a brilliant approach: "I called the CTO [Chief Technology Officer] and talked him into letting me send around our primary technology guru." That went well, which made the next step even easier: setting up the technology guru with the senior leadership team. "We sent him around to train the executive assistants. That was a cool move. Now they've set up their own network group, they're staying in touch, they're working together."

And if there's anybody a busy executive will stop long enough to get a computer tip from, it's his admin. Brilliant!

> The work flow between individuals makes them more productive, makes them more valuable, gets things done faster.

Dave provided another example of technology bringing a productivity benefit, but this one represents a benefit for customers—

Today if you go to a service station and they don't have the electronic payment option, do you stay and walk into the office to pay for your gas, or do you drive off and look for another station? Electronic payment has become table stakes in the marketplace. If you want to be in business today, you've got to have pay-at-the-pump.

At Chevron, we were the first company to use satellites for that technology. When you go to a Chevron station and you stick your card in at the pump, a miracle occurs. The digits from the card are received at the pump, they're transmitted into the station, where a computer takes that data stream and beams it up onto the roof to an antenna. The antenna sends those digits out to a geosynchronous satellite, which bounces the signal back down to corporate headquarters in San Ramon, California, where it's fed into a fiber pipe that runs to Sacramento. There a mainframe computer does a full credit authorization. When the transaction is authorized, a signal traces back along the same path, back down to the pump. And how long does that take on average? Between two and three seconds; up to five seconds if it's not a Chevron card. And I call that my little miracle.

Chevron led the way with that in the early 1990s, taking a risk on this expensive technology, with the marketing people pushing for it, and we developed the way to do it. They were sure it would be a differentiator. And until everybody else got onto it, what a differentiator it was!

Of course, no one guarantees that every technology effort will pay off. In the ever-changing financial market, Lloyds Bank has suffered that problem. Archie Kane remarked:

To be perfectly honest, my perception is that we've had varied benefits and varied values from our technology investment—to downright no value whatsoever. Some of the failures were in the dot-com related areas. And some were in the areas of business initiative efforts that amounted to nothing because the market moved on.

But the range goes all the way through to others that have given us clear value of money.

Even the efforts that don't work out represent part of the investment in leveraging technology for competitive advantage. The challenge lies in recognizing those limited opportunities to do something that differentiates you from the competition purely with technology—

> It's a constant focus to continually look at the business model for places where I can streamline processes. It's all about the business model, it's not about the technology.

Beyond Productivity Improvement: the Third Wave

ChevronTexaco's Dave Clementz has a vision of how all this extends into the future:

> The next big wave, the third wave, comes about when groups start talking to each other about working in the white space between them. And that's when business innovation occurs. The models begin to change.
>
> When people are familiar with the technology tools, they start bringing forward suggestions. That triggers business management to start seeing opportunities they hadn't spotted before, and they begin asking the right kind of questions: 'Why are we doing it this way?' 'Why do we still have this hand process of passing these invoices through?' 'What if we could do this on the network automatically?' 'What if we could create a central database where all the information streams into and then we all feed off that central database so we don't have different data flowing around?'

The third wave arrives when people start to do business integration—a coming benefit of technology we can all look forward to.

Take-Aways

The principal message of this chapter is simple to state, and simple (if demanding) to put into practice: the leader of the business and his or her direct reports need to be intimately engaged in the decisions about the implementation of information technology. Only through this level of involvement can a company have any realistic chance of reaping a significant return from the increasing investments being made in technology.

This is not a new point. I and others have been beating a drum about the need for years. Yet as the interviews here reveal, senior executives will admit that they have not been much engaged in the process.

Linked to this is a point we made in *Driving Digital*—the requirement that senior executives become ardent users of technology themselves. How else can anyone comprehend and appreciate the issues involved? And not just becoming literate about technology, but becoming personally engaged in all significant IT investments.

Maybe every corporate executive should be framing a small placard to hang on the wall, or creating a reminder that pops up on his or her computer once a month, that says something like:

STAY INTIMATELY INVOLVED IN TECHNOLOGY DECISIONS OR FORGET ABOUT ACHIEVING A TECHNOLOGY RETURN ON INVESTMENT.

3

You're Using Technology in Support of Business Processes — Right?

> I had this one guy say, "You know, I used to run all this on a big tablet, I could still do it today, I don't need your stinkin' computers."
>
> — Steve Hankins, *CFO, Tyson Foods*

In bygone days when "computer" meant mainframe, a data printout got plunked down on your desk by the in-house mail guy as a several-inch-high stack on a continuous-form paper, maybe a hundred or a few hundred sheets with tear-away perforations along each side. At the same time that we acknowledge how revolutionary and highly valuable this was, we still chuckle at how primitive it now seems.

Today we laud the computer for its contributions to productivity and convenience. But I find too many people who think productivity and convenience alone are enough to justify technology, and fail to notice the gulf that too often divides the business people from the technology folks.

The issue boils down to this: how can an organization bring greater understanding between the business side of the house and the technology side? How can you make certain that technology is being used as an enabler for business processes?

To put it another way: how do you go about changing the way your people think about technology?

The following are stories of companies that have been, in the words of the shop-worn expression, "thinking outside the box." To me, stories like this are an inspiration.

The Age-Old Problem of the Old Age Manager

At Tyson Foods, even though they already have a process in place and a good level of understanding from the business side, Stan Hankins made clear that not all the managers have signed on—

> We had this one man from the business side a few years back. His unit desperately needed some new technology, but he told me, 'You know, I used to run all this on a big tablet, I could still do it today, I don't need your stinkin' computers.'
>
> All the people who worked for him knew that they needed this technology. They were the ones who had the process issues and such. We went ahead with the project, and those people were really involved. They understood the need and the benefit, so they were glad to come to the party.
>
> Today a lot of those same people have now moved up to higher levels. That's what I refer to as 'management transition.'

So when Steve was using the underlings of a refusnik as allies to get a project done, he was at the same time laying a foundation by getting the underlings indoctrinated to the philosophy and the process. As they moved up, they took those attitudes with them.

But often, you don't have to wait for people to retire or get forced out—

> What we found is you don't have to do anything to change those hang-back managers, they'll change themselves. Once some of those people figure out, 'This world is changing, and this change is bigger than me,' many times they move out on their own. We've really not ever had any situation where for technology reasons we had to make a case for changing someone in a more senior position.
>
> It often happens on its own with what I call the 'surround and conquer' strategy—coming at them with their own people pulling from below and top management pushing from above, while we urge on the players any way we can.
>
> But not always. For example, with the warehouse managers, we realized quickly that some weren't going to be warehouse managers anymore.

As Steve describes it, the management of Tyson Foods has learned the need to "raise the level of the intellectual game to achieve benefits."

Applying Technology Process in the Real World

At Airborne, before the company became part of DHL, an effort they call 'the Phoenix project' showed another face of IT taking responsibility for recognizing a business need. Airborne's Rachelle Mileur described it as a strategic project for the company, aimed at improving the back-office processes while at the same time servicing the sales force to provide better customer support. When we spoke, the project was still in its early stages—

> From a priority standpoint, we elected to attack the sales force need first with the tools around the Internet. Secondly, we hadn't really invested in improving our supply chain systems in quite a while; we had old technology that was getting very difficult to maintain, and costly. And there were silos of systems that were making it even more difficult not only to manage, but also maintain from a systems stand-point. So we felt we certainly needed to replace these aging systems.

This is a splendid example of what I'm always looking for: an IT group on the prowl for ways to fix things that people in the business units haven't even complained about. Yet.

But Rachelle wasn't finished with her list of problems the Phoenix project was tackling—

> In many cases we were doing things manually. So another goal of the project aims to replace a lot of paper shuffling. For every repetitive task we can automate, we allow an employee to work either on something more strategic, or something that requires more analysis and use of information.

To me, that sounds pretty much like a definition of turning knowledge workers into information workers, (which we address in the following chapter). She continued—

> This was mostly a software matter, but certainly we wanted to make process changes where those were needed. Many processes are going to change so the systems are no longer siloed. And right now there are forty different inventory systems; when we're done, there will be one single view of the inventory. That will help facilitate the business process change, as well.

Deploying technology to solve business problems proceeds in gradual steps. Sometimes, says Lloyds's Archie Kane, progress can seem to be more gradual than we'd like—

> We've done some great work on customer information systems that we've deployed in customer facing positions that have improved our loan generation capability and our ability to sell and service customers. We've got a very good operational customer information system that pulls together core data. We've built a good infrastructure, which helps us have better information about our customer and understand the customer needs better.
>
> So there are a number of areas where we have really helped move things forward from the business perspective. There are also examples where I think that we can point to the deployment of technology as part of a series of productivity projects. That would be in things like deployment of workflow. You take a real customer need where you've got high transactional throughput and you say, 'We want to reengineer that.'
>
> Now is it all brilliant? Absolutely not. Even though it's already given us real advantage, there's still a lot that we have to do to leverage this capability.

To one Army civilian executive, the battle for change takes the form of an effort to find solutions to problems of consolidation. The speaker is Joe Capps, the Army's Director of Enterprise Systems Technology Activity—

> Just as there is an enterprise push across corporate America, we're taking a very similar approach from a business case perspective, looking for solutions that are consolidated and applied across all Army customers.
>
> The intent is that we will capture the requirements across the Army, as opposed to having multiple Army organizations developing their individual solutions. By doing that, we aim to prevent duplication of effort. A very simple but obvious example is that you don't want to have a server that's underutilized at one location, and nearby have a second server procured by another organization that's also underutilized. You should be able to consolidate the use of those two and only own one server.
>
> We're going to have a continuum, a permanent capability interface with the customer to insure that we're meeting their

requirements. And if we aren't, then there will be a process in place for them to alert us so we can address that issue.

For metrics, we're establishing a measurement of whether we're successfully meeting a customer's requirements. That means measuring things like number of outages, how long outages last, how deep into their building we have to go, whether or not we're actually providing connectivity to all of their customers, and so on. If we don't meet any of those metrics, there's a process by which the customer can flag it.

Joe explained that for non-critical activities, the Army doesn't expect to stay on the leading edge of technology, but chooses to lag behind—

If you don't do an enterprise solution, what you have is like a mob that's running along behind, some of them three steps behind, some of them thirty steps behind—very disjointed. If you take an enterprise systems approach, then you move the entire crowd up to exactly three steps behind industry

So that's one thing we get from an enterprise solution. We get to keep up with what we call the 'trailing edge of technology,' and we do so all at the same time, not disjointed.

Internal customers tend to be more or less the same everywhere—even within a military organization—

People think their needs are unique to them, and they're the only person in the world who has that problem. Usually it's not quite as unique as the person thinks it is.

That's the whole point of an enterprise solution. You find a solution that's common enough to meet multiple people's requirements, but still flexible enough to meet slight variations.

A lot of companies could take a page from the playbook of the U.S. Army when it comes to providing an enterprise-wide solution while still making it possible to tailor individual installations to meet the distinctive needs of each unit of the organization.

Evolution in a Company's Use of Technology

In the previous chapter, we talked about technology at the small pallet remanufacturing firm called East Industries. Founder David Wilson provided some backstory of how they got to where they are

today that offers another perspective on using technology to pre-
cipitate change:

> About fifteen years ago, we were growing and we needed to
> establish some sort of accounting program customized to
> each customer. I realized with the advent of computers that
> all of our accounting was eventually going to be electronic,
> so we got started with Lotus. Eventually companies became
> more sophisticated and realized there was money to be saved
> if they could sell their pallets, or get credit for them, or
> reuse them.
>
> We kept developing more specific customer programs, but
> in that process we also needed to have the big picture for our-
> selves because it's hard to measure apples, bananas, and
> peaches, and come out with a bottom line for the company.

That was the motivation for hiring their outside computer consultant, who has been helping the company ever since—

> We began to realize that a lot of the managers we were dealing
> with [at our customer's companies] seemed to be very happy
> because our accounting and record keeping alleviated prob-
> lems of them having to spend their labor and time in keeping
> up with everything.

That was striking, because some of the customers who were so
impressed by East's technology were much larger companies.
Meanwhile, Dave Wilson recognized East Industries was setting a
standard in this area—

> The reports we delivered had a professional look with profes-
> sional accountability, and were just as much a part of the pack-
> age as was the service side of the business. We were so far
> ahead of the competitors that a lot of them are not around
> anymore.
>
> The powerful thing about technology for us as a small busi-
> ness is that it allows us to spend more time in front of our cus-
> tomer, and not worry about bean counting in the back room,
> because that's being take care of.

Meanwhile, as the economy slowed and business grew leaner,
their accounting program allowed the company to exercise better
control of their own business—

In the last year, we've been disassembling 1,200 to 1,500 pallets a day, utilizing component parts, resizing and reusing the wood, and all of that. We've now tied all of this data into the program, as well, getting us to a bottom-line number. And that became essential—because the business had grown but margins were thinner and thinner, so I had no other way; there really was no other way to manage it.

Keeping Projects from Getting into Trouble

If your company has already achieved a heads-up stance about using technology as a tool for process change, you have good reason to feel self-satisfied. But change is never a good thing when it comes at too high a price. How great a job are you doing when it comes to catching on that some new project is in trouble? And do you have a mechanism in place to do something about it?

GMAC-RFC's Rick Greenwood commented, "You have to change the organization so that it becomes okay to say, 'This is not right to go forward with.'" And then he added, "I'm not saying we've achieved that yet, but we're starting to get it into place." Still, as always, recognizing the need is the first step.

Head of the Wachovia Bank's eCommerce Division, and an Executive Vice President, is Lawrence Baxter, whose credentials may seem surprising for a man in a key technology position: he holds undergraduate degrees in business and law, and a Ph.D. that combines the fields of law and government regulation. Lawrence offered some insight into the bank's approach on assessing tech projects—

> One of our most common challenges is that we have to try to size all projects at such an early stage, in order to stop them from going too far in terms of company commitment of expenditure. And so a lot of the subsequent adjustments have to do with a mixture not just of dilatoriness or imperfect execution, but really of discovery.
>
> When you take on a project, it often turns out to be much more difficult than you ever imagined or that anybody in the industry might have imagined. Sometimes I look back and think we're in such a fog of the unknown that it's a miracle we actually get anything done on budget and on time at all.

Particularly with initiatives that involve innovation of any kind, we increasingly ask outside consulting firms when they bid, 'Have you done this before? If you have, please show us what you've done.' If not, we don't want to do the project with them because we've learned that there's so much discovery required, they don't bring the help to us we need. That atmosphere of 'exploration' generates a negative dynamic, and people become very skeptical of any new project even if it would obviously save the company enormous amounts of money. The attitude is, 'Well, we haven't seen this done before, and we all know what happens when you embark on something that you're confident is going to save us money but you've not done before.'

Lawrence points out other problems, as well, when a consulting firm is running a large technology project for your company—

The centers of activity are very scattered and the people change over time, so the accountability can become very quickly diffused. You have to have a focused, warrior culture to be able to sustain accountability over time.

We try to keep good people in critical positions so their expertise and institutional memory is not lost. But frankly, that's talking out of both sides of our mouths because we also talk about making sure we provide opportunities for career development. Of course, the skeptic will complain, 'You found a person who knew what they were doing in their job and you moved the person out of that job as soon as you could because that's called advancement.'

It's a familiar problem we've all encountered. And certainly a bigger problem, as Lawrence pointed out, when it happens in the middle of a major project push. Lawrence's term for these types of problems is "the trap of the mundane."

Any leader or manager serious about holding his own feet to the fire can't escape taking on the responsibility for projects gone bad. All of us have those in our history. Lawrence comments, "There are some projects about which I would hate to have the judgment come down upon me. I'd like to claim I inherited them, but the truth is at some point you've got to say, 'Well, I beat around the bush on this project long enough, but I can't blame anybody else, I should have stopped it earlier. It's on my shoulders.'"

Taking IT Through a Corporate Merger

In 2001, Texaco and Chevron merged to form a $44 billion company, becoming the third largest U.S. producer of oil and gas. For IT, pulling together the technologies of two companies in a merger or acquisition brings a ten-gallon headache of trying to integrate their computer networks, e-mail, and all the rest; putting together two giants can be the mother of all headaches. That's what Dave Clementz faced when he went from being the IT boss of Chevron to being the IT super-boss of the combined companies.

A merger challenges IT on many levels. Dave offered a run-down of what he now sees, looking back, as the most memorable IT lessons for surviving a large-scale merger—

> One thing that was the key to the success, and a crucial element to the speed with which we were able to do the integration, was having a really strong upfront merger team specifically for IT.
>
> The Merger Integration Team started about nine months before the merger. They did all the planning, looked at all the systems that had to be merged, and came up with 125 projects that had to be synchronized. When it's done right and it works, you know that it's been synchronized.
>
> Another key was setting the governance model through the CIO Council. If I hadn't had a CIO Council, there's no way in hell I could have done it with those 125 projects going on at once all over the company.
>
> Keeping people focused on the job I think proved to be one of the most essential ingredients.

Despite the rigorous planning, Clementz knew there would also be plenty of unpleasant surprises—

> The main issue, I think, you could put into a category called change management. I just didn't anticipate how much the change management issue itself was going to impact performance during that period.
>
> We had this thing wired. Day One we threw the switch and the companies could communicate, the networks were connected, people were talking, communicating, getting e-mail, connected to the private networks. Day Two, still home and alive. About one week later is when things started to be problematic.

As soon as the first executive moved from Texas to California and changed domains, now they had two e-mail boxes and the confusion of two different message systems.

At that point, we had a lot of well meaning people who tried to cowboy things—stepping in to find a fix and not realizing, 'If I meddle with this, it's going to affect that.' When everything is connected to everything else, you gain the advantages of saving money and being able to communicate better, but it's bad in the sense that you mess up when people start trying to do little local fixes.

The answer is to put into place this rigorous change management discipline. There were no catastrophic events, nothing really serious. There were just a lot of little things that I think would have been big ones but for this change management effort. And a lot of little ones that could have been avoided altogether if we had been more demanding about the change management.

Overall, the merger was a notable success, and Dave sounds proud when he talks about it—

In about a year and a half following the merger, we captured about a quarter of a billion dollars through synergy. These were savings from the total costs that the two IT organizations had [previously] had together. When you get everybody together and start integrating processes, integrating the software, getting leverage from combined licenses, and so forth, we were able to squeeze $250 million out of the ongoing operational cost of the combined IT organization.

Training as a Technology-Based Process

Say the words "technology" and "change" in the same sentence, and at some companies you're likely to find the subject of internal education popping into the conversation. That's certainly the case if the guy you're talking to is Gary Moore, a senior vice president at Cisco Systems, Inc. You quickly catch on that he sees this as a hot topic; he admits that "e-learning is actually one of my favorite things to talk about."

Putting an e-learning capability into Cisco was really driven out of necessity. That happened when Cisco went from router product and moved into all of these other areas, like switching, Internet telephony, and security. We were going through product changes very rapidly. An e-learning application was developed to be the communication tool for addressing issues like how do we sell and position these new investments. And that drove the investment.

E-learning is widely used in the company now. With products changing so fast, it's had to keep our systems engineers, technical engineers, and field organization up to speed with everything. Guess the first thing engineers do when they sign on for an online course? They take the test, and then they say, 'I need to study chapters one, four, six and nine.' They do that, then they take the test again, and pass, and they move on. It's no longer, 'You have to start at point A and go through point Z before you can take the test.'

The other thing that we see is they don't do this during the day, when the company would like to see them out with customers. They do it at home at night, 2 o'clock in the morning. It's really wild to see the times people are signing on to take these courses. In fact, our productivity using e-learning didn't go up until we understood that this was the learning process our employees needed and desired.

Another example brought e-learning to the attention of a great many people at Cisco—

When Cisco was recertifying for [the quality management standard] ISO 9000, in 2001, the company had twelve weeks to get some additional training done. The plan called for a bunch of people going around from city to city, and the price tag was $4 million. That cost was an issue, but the training was essential because the certification is essential to Cisco's positioning. Even so, there was a more important issue: they couldn't get it done in twelve weeks.

The company solved that problem by putting the training on the network, for a much smaller cost. Rather than spending $4 million, we spent less than $10,000. And they didn't just get the training done by the deadline; they got it done in half the time—six weeks.

An impressive story. But is it a lesson in using e-learning, or is there a bigger message here about using the network for collaboration?

There are a lot of collaboration tools that you can use, not just to run your meetings, but also to teach classes and to get education out to your entire company. We have Video on Demand. We have courses where an instructor is doing training over the Internet and interacting with the students.

There's a tremendous capability with e-learning but you need to have the infrastructure and that gets back to the value proposition. It's not about reducing costs, it's about coming up with a value proposition of, 'Why do I need integrative voice, video, and data?' Where it's justified, it's justified because it supports employee services and customer care.

Also, our customers can go into our website and try to sort through a problem that they're having. Anytime they want, they click a button and they're connected to a live Cisco engineer. Being a technology company, of course we have a lot more capability than many other companies, but we're very open in sharing this with our customers and helping them to be successful.

The philosophy here is in helping our customers use the power of the network and the power of the Internet, to change the future of their company.

Barcode Tags and Letterheads

There are any number of stories in these pages about hundred-million-dollar technology projects, and even one of the smaller company CEOs talks about a project that he chose to do despite the fact that for the same cost he could have hired two full-time employees.

But sometimes a stunning technology project can come in the form of a tiny item that hardly seems significant enough to make a difference, as made clear in this story from the Army's Carla von Bernewitz:

Most people have heard about how in Desert Storm we had all these cargo ships arrive and we had no clue what was in each container. We now have a technology that enables us to know what's in each container and know that we've got the guns or bullets or food we need, and exactly where it's located.

They call the process "automated identification technology"— nothing more than adhesive barcode tags that they slap on when the containers are being loaded. A small item, but in any fast-response military operation they now make an enormous difference when the goods are landed in the battle zone.

Another example of ingenuity offered by Carla that I want to include here, even though it's not a technology project; still, it struck me as a further reminder that worthwhile efforts don't have to be on a grand scale—

> There are any number of ways that we have for putting new ideas on the table. We have something called, interestingly enough, the Business Initiatives Council, which is more or less a modern version of the old factory suggestion box—a way of inviting proposals for improving operations.
>
> One of the proposals that came to them, a simple one, was eliminating printed letterhead. Think of the usual process—the procurement people or contracting folks who buy it for you, the receiving clerks who log the boxes in when they arrive, the warehouse clerks who stored it, the shipping clerks who get it for you when you need some, and then the admin who gets a sheet of the letterhead paper and loads it into the printer when you're ready to go.

Point well taken. Some of us are beyond that already, but obviously there are some organizations that have hung on longer to tradition—

> The suggestion of everyone creating their own letterhead as stationery in their word processing program, and printing out letters and memos on plain paper, was one of the things that went through the Business Initiatives Council. It was approved very quickly, and that's what we're doing today. And it turned out to account for a huge dollar savings.

Take-Aways

Technology itself can't bring about change. When new technology is being installed and processes need to change, management has to step up to that responsibility. (And throughout the book, we'll be looking at various aspects of project management and leadership responsibility.)

Some companies choose and install technology first, and then start looking at the impact. Wrong. Technology decisions need to be driven by intimate knowledge of the business process, with technology solutions chosen only after careful, reasoned analysis of how successful they are likely to be for solving a business problem.

Acting in its traditional role, IT has usually waited for requests from the business side—a responsive model. Instead, an IT group should know that it is expected to take a more pro-active role: staying alert to the needs of the business units, recognizing problems that a technology solution might be able to provide an answer for, and proposing those solutions to the business leader. The IT group should not be a bunch of mechanics with a variety of tools and spare parts, but a problem-solving organization.

By now most companies have an established mechanism in place for authorizing and prioritizing major technology projects. But how this is actually done at different companies makes for a fascinating comparison, with lessons for us all. Coming up next: making the business case for technology and justifying the technology spend.

PART TWO

Making the Business Case for Technology

4

Making the Business Case for Technology, I: Justifying the Technology Spend

People's yardstick for value too often focuses on measuring productivity in terms of their current processes, rather than looking at technology as a catalyst for radically rethinking how you do things.

— Steve Hankins, *CFO, Tyson Foods*

Who owns the major IT projects—should it be IT, or should it be the business side?

I think the answer to that question ought to be obvious. Ultimately, someone has to be held accountable for generating the profits, the revenues, and the productivity gain—and that "someone" needs to be on the business side. Too often the IT group is the one called on to own the cost benefit study for IT efforts, or else after the fact gets hammered for not cost justifying, when this obligation really belongs on the shoulders of the business side.

We sometimes forget the obvious truth that technology provides no benefit of its own; it's the *application* of technology that produces ROI. This chapter explores aspects of this question, which is one of the core issues addressed in this book

Forging a Strong Relationship Between IT and the Business Units

At Tyson Foods, it's long been the practice to make business people part of all major technology projects. As CFO Steve Hankins put it,

"We have always planted business people within the technology project teams." And he added an important caveat: "But in today's world, on our major technology efforts, the business actually leads the project. All major projects have a business leader who's formally appointed."

In my view, as you've gathered by now, the "single owner" of a major technology project should be some senior person from the business unit who requested the project or capability in the first place, and who will lead the developmental and implementation effort. So I couldn't help noticing Steve's assessment that "the business actually leads the process." *Actually,* as if he's surprised that this has come to be the case. Yet Tyson Foods is doing so many things right in the area of technology culture that their success shouldn't come as a surprise.

At least they already have the attitude right; Steve Hankins observed—

> There's a big effort to be sure that these are viewed as business projects, not technology projects. On smaller projects, the person who has the business responsibility regarding the project doesn't necessarily become a full-time project lead.
>
> But the IT department uses business relationship managers who interface with all the areas of the business, and it's between the relationship manager and the business head that the priority list is managed. And so whatever is being worked on, the overwhelming odds are it's because the business leader made that decision. It's not IT back in some dark room making the decision.

At this point in the conversation, I sounded the drum for one of my main themes on this subject—the one that says having the IT group own the business case is illogical since, ultimately, the business leader of the affected organization really controls the assets and resources that have got to change if you're going to get the benefits you want. Steve responded—

> That's exactly right. It's something we grew to over a number of years. In the early '90s, I couldn't necessarily get a business leader to own a business case around some things. We began to push ahead with that view anyway, and we created a case on project after project that convinced them to take more and

more of a role. So today, the business people take a very strong role around these things.

I would have trouble believing that that's something an organization suddenly changes. I think that you probably have to grow into that because—I'll be honest with you—here it's sometimes taken a change in management to accomplish this.

One approach Tyson Foods adopted in convincing business-unit leaders to step up to the plate sounds like a sure winner—

We made certain the business leaders were involved in the process. So even if they weren't exactly eager to take a business leadership role, we treated them like they were. If they didn't want to have a status meeting, then we still had one—and they would come. And we constantly would put them in the position of being the leader. When somebody didn't want to do the presentation to senior management, we'd write it and hand it to them. We would do whatever it took, but our goal was try to get them on stage.

I would talk with senior management of the business unit and say, 'Okay, when we get in there, we need this guy to take ownership, so you've got to pin him on the wall on that.' And they would. So we sort of drove some people to it.

But one of my philosophies was that you needed to get people to live through technology projects, have an appreciation for how the process works, and come to understand why what to a lot of people seems to be such a minutely detailed level really can make a huge difference when the technology starts being used by their people.

I believe you've got to get a lot of people from this 50,000-foot view down into the trenches.

The Tyson people found that after one of their business unit leaders lived through a project, he would behave much differently on the next. Having gained an understanding of why things are done the way they are, the person assumes ownership on a completely different level. As Steve Hankins puts it, "Growth takes place."

Integris Health stands at a different point on the curve: they appreciate the need but are still trying to make it happen. We asked to what extent the business side is involved in technology projects being done for them, and Integris CEO Stan Hupfeld described the current attitudes at the company:

Actually we're just in the process of trying to do this better than we've done it in the past. There are things we probably haven't done as well as we should, but we're trying to start.

Number one is insuring that our operational people have ownership of the technology and the implementation of the technology. Far too often it becomes an IT issue and IT either succeeds or fails, and they're either castigated or applauded based on that.

Because we haven't had much oversight in the past, we've had some issues where the operators just kind of disassociate themselves from IT and if something doesn't work, it's not their fault. That's what we're trying to get away from.

And so we're trying to reverse our thinking to where, for a technology project, it's simply a utility to the operating folks. We're creating an internal board composed of our senior operators. The IT Director will report to that board. We also have a big board-level committee, but the Director will have an internal board of operators who will assist him in building the business case for new technology. We'll review his budgets, both capital and operating. We'll develop the plans for the implementation of the new technologies and insure that it meets our business plan.

The leadership of Washington Mutual has found a way to make reporting on major technology projects an integral part of the business review process. CIO Jerry Gross—

Each quarter I sit through all the business reviews where technology is just embedded within their performance reporting. This does a couple of good things. One is that they have total ownership and skin in the game in these projects, and they view them as part of their portfolio with all of their other projects.

The skin in the game comes from the fact that each of the business-unit leaders—for example, the president of the banking business—has her direct reports sitting around the table; one of them is a technology person who also reports into me. Now there's a hard line reporting into me and a dotted line reporting into her, but she considers that individual to be part of her team. So that person attends the meetings once a week and is part of the strategic planning and the business planning, and receives all of their business project priorities.

That person's performance is evaluated on how well he or she is synchronizing with the business—that's about 40 percent of his/her performance evaluation. The rest of it is whether they're deploying technology that is standardized, consistent with the corporation, cost effective, of value, etc. Those metrics flow up to me, whereas customer satisfaction and synchronizing with the business, those metrics flow up to the business.

Now, a lot of this is easier said than done. And it takes a tremendous amount of lobbying and persuasion in the enterprise to pull it off. It's also one of these things that's like, 'What have you done for me lately?' Just because you've done well for a period of time doesn't mean that past success will be an indicator of future success. So it's a constant synchronization and managing of the relationship.

The quarterly business reviews and the Capital Expenditures Committee are key pieces to the success. The IT organization in many companies is viewed as a service bureau, or purely as a cost center—'Just keep the lights on and oh, by the way, I'll tell you what else I need from you.' And then the IT organization goes away and delivers on those needs.

Think of these efforts as forging relationships and building bridges of understanding.

Getting the Business Side to Take Ownership of Technology

Part of the disconnect between the business side and IT revolves around a question of where the money is coming from. As Marsh Inc.'s Roger Smith sees it, sometimes managers see the size of the IT budget, and don't understand why their pet project isn't being funded—

As we became larger, we had to increase our budget on infrastructure. In the past, during a fiscal year a business segment would say, 'You know, we really, really need a [Customer Relationship Management] product,' or whatever, and IT had to say, 'We hear you, we agree with you, we understand, we'd love to do it, we don't have the money.'

'Why don't you have the money?'

'Well, because we have to keep your servers running and your e-mail, and all that's important, right? That's what we're spending the money on.'

Some of this is growth and some of this is smart use of resources; we can accommodate the former and we have learned how to better manage the latter.

It's one thing to agree that the business case for a technology project should belong to the business side. Sometimes, though, getting the business unit leaders to step up to the plate proves more difficult than it's supposed to be. What then?

I was fascinated with the way one IT executive forced a management team into action—and this story comes not from the corporate world but from the military, making it an even better lesson. At the time, Carla von Bernewitz was CIO of the Defense Logistics Agency (in governmentese, the DLA), and found herself saddled with legacy systems as much as forty years old, including ancient operating systems and an unsupported version of COBOL—

I was hearing the field commanders say that they couldn't do Just-in-Time inventory management, they couldn't do ordering off the Web, they couldn't do this, they couldn't do that, they couldn't do something else—because their systems wouldn't allow it.

So with the concurrence of the leadership, I set up a conference and hauled all these generals and senior executive staff members out to the desert. I went through an educational process to show these business unit leaders that there were other ways of accomplishing what they wanted to do, and there were other ways of supporting their businesses with newer systems. I really didn't care what technology they picked as long as it wasn't forty years old and unsupported, so they would no longer be able to say, 'I can't do it because my system won't let me.'

The reason I took them to the desert was because there was a software company out there that was able to wrap the old stuff inside new technology. That was very appealing to [the DLA field commanders] because it meant they didn't have to change, they didn't have to get rid of their old stuff.

They didn't move very quickly, but eventually these people came to the decision that they really did need to get a new system, that they needed to get rid of their forty-year-old systems. They wanted to do a lot of the direct vendor delivery and so on that everybody else was doing. DLA really did want their systems to be able to go into the field with their customers—the

Army, Navy, and Air Force—and they didn't want to kluge things together off of hardcopy reports to get the information for making business decisions.

So they decided to go forward with a procurement, and they made their own selection of technology. They chose the systems implementer, and they looked at every [Enterprise Resource Planning] vendor out there and selected the one they thought would best support their business practices.

I thought that it was great for a CIO to get the business people to make decisions like that. I was really happy about it.

Asked what the secret was to getting a group of non-technical executives to make these technology decisions, Carla offered her formula. "I put them in the driver's seat," she said. "Every two weeks we gathered for an offsite, which I and my people managed intensely. But it was the business units that were driving it." She also followed the standard of "always having the cost of making any particular decision separated out from other projects they had under way."

One other guideline Ms. von Bernewitz insisted on was, if I recall correctly, a management principle of President Eisenhower: she said she made sure they understood that "deciding not to make a decision was also a decision."

Summing up, she says: "It was making sure that it was the business units responsible for the decision making—putting them in the driver's seat—that made the difference."

Measuring Business Value

In evaluating proposed technology projects, companies use the full range of financial measures—net present value, and internal rate of return, and the rest. But in the view of Steve Hankins, "People's yardstick for value too often focus on measuring productivity in terms of their current processes rather than looking at technology as a catalyst for radically rethinking how you do things."

Steve gave a sample of the kinds of questions he'd like to see people in his company paying more attention to: "How do you think we at Tyson, from a business leadership perspective, should look at assessing technology value? What approach should we take to try to determine what if any value accrues as a result of investing in information technology?"

But what about a project that looks good at first and then doesn't measure up? Is a project ever cut back in scale or changed in some way because it becomes clear that the promised savings or increased revenue, or whatever the other promises were, don't look as if they are actually going to be realized? At insurance broker Marsh, according to Roger Smith, this is not an uncommon occurrence—

> There are different phases early in the process where we can decide whether to proceed or not, and we are continually balancing the demand for technology solutions. As an insurance broker and risk consultant, our customer base is in the hundreds of thousands. But our business segments present very different technology solutions—for example, serving a global services company as opposed to a single location manufacturer. Some of the applications that could be enterprise wide might only affect 3,000 customers. And sometimes the development cost is such that there just isn't enough improvement over the way we're doing things now, or there's not a demand.
>
> So many times we delve into a proposed technology solution, start to work on it, noodle it around, and then decide that it's a very good thing, but we're not going to do it this year.
>
> The whole goal is to get an early start, plan it as much as we can, and then keep it on track. There will be one or two projects a year that get pulled back; either something else takes priority or there's just a change in emphasis.
>
> A strong and sustaining element throughout this development process is 'the voice of the customer.' We ask similar questions as we do when designing a risk solution for a customer: will this enable our customer to meet their goals and objectives?

Roger describes projects at Marsh as occasionally reaching the point where "In spite of all the planning, we just say, 'It's not working.' This may happen in the development stage when someone realizes, 'We thought we could do this for a million but it's going to be three million.' The other point is where costs are in line, development times are in line, but we get it out in pilot and everybody says, 'It's really, really great but it's just not doing what we thought it would do.' And that may be enough to cancel."

And sometimes a project gets into trouble because it was started based on a "keeping up with the Jones's" rationale—

Are we doing this because our competitors are doing it? Sometimes that is a valid, acceptable business reason, and it's fine. But what do you do with, 'Our biggest competitor has this, we have to have it, it's going to cost $10 million!' I often tell people, 'You can do the wrong thing for the right reason.'

At root, the question of measuring the business value of technology can call for a change in attitudes and thinking patterns.

I remember doing work with Hewlett-Packard some years ago, and we were trying to define the difference between 'effectiveness' and 'efficiency.' 'Efficiency' usually gets boiled down to productivity issues we're all used to measuring. The 'effectiveness' piece is the really tricky one. That, I think, is the heart of some of the frustration many people have about determining the right measure going forward. If you could figure out how to measure the improved effectiveness of an employee after installing new technology, that would be of real value to a company.

Productivity: an Academic View

The need for a better understanding of productivity was raised by Lee Schlenker, a French-American on the faculty of the École de Management of Lyon, in southern France, who is also a business consultant to companies including Oracle, Microsoft, and SAP—

> The real failure of judging information technology isn't just in *what* we measure but in how we measure. Management hasn't come to grips with how tough it is to actually measure what business value is.
>
> I would take it one step further and suggest that you have to be careful of the measuring stick that you're using. This measuring stick is evolving—we're no longer measuring productivity as we did in the 1920s and 30s, where companies were essentially built around factories producing physical goods. When we're talking about collaboration, for example, we're looking at a whole different set of measurements. Management really needs to come to grips with taking a close look at how they want to measure where their firm is going.
>
> Once those measures are decided upon, to get the payoff is going to result, in many cases, in having to drive change forward—rethinking business processes, rethinking organization structures to focus on meeting client demands for quality,

timeliness, service, trust, and so on. No matter how you measure it, only if that occurs are you going to get some benefit.

Schlenker maintains that there is a relationship issue, as well—

Whether we're implementing ERP systems, or supply chain systems, or even CRM systems, we're focusing on incremental improvements in processes, we're talking about efficiency. When you ask a businessman, 'Forget about technology and talk to me about what helps make a sale,' he or she focuses on the effectiveness of the relationship that the people have with their team, they have with their company, they have with their clients or their markets. This notion of effectiveness is something that's measured very poorly.

Looking for a Way to Measure Productivity

As it turns out, a serious effort in this direction is already underway. Not long ago, Bill Gates was speaking at an industry conference and made a statement to the effect that Microsoft would be producing software that would allow companies to double their productivity. When he repeated it not long after to some major customers in Detroit, he was asked, "But, Bill, how would we measure that?"

Bill brought the question back to Microsoft headquarters in Redmond, Washington. And then Jeff Raikes got the same question at a Microsoft CEO Summit when he made a similar comment. (A long-time Microsoft stalwart, Jeff is currently responsible for one-third of company revenues; his title is Group Vice President, Productivity and Business Services. And he has been my boss almost the entire time I've worked here.)

People at the company looked into the subject and found that nobody seemed to have an answer to the question of how an organization can measure the productivity of its knowledge workers. The company decided this was an issue that American industry could benefit from having some specific answers to, and Microsoft was willing to put up resources to get an effort started, forming a group that would be called the Information Work Productivity Council. Susan Conway, Ph.D., is now running the effort, with Jeff Raikes as Chairman. Susan brings to the position a background in resource allocation and technical project management, and extensive experience at companies such as Texaco and NCR before joining Microsoft.

As the title suggests, the focus is not on what has come to be called "knowledge workers." A paper issued by the Council, *Productivity Evolution* (available in full on their website, iwproductivity.org), explains that 'knowledge work' is "a somewhat elitist term, generally restricted to highly-paid scientists and engineers, professionals and managers." The Council sees knowledge work as a subset of *information* work, which they envision as covering a much broader occupational category of people who create, manage, share, receive, or manipulate information.

To use an example that Susan Conway likes to cite, the interstate trucker, equipped with his Global Positioning System hardware for location, his cell phone for communications, and maybe a palm-top with his schedule and load information—he, too, is an information worker. So is the lathe operator or tool-maker, who gets his instruction from some kind of computer-based communications device, and feeds back data on what tasks he has completed.

Data from the U.S. Bureau of Labor Statistics suggests that "nearly 70 percent of the 136 million employees in the U.S. non-farm workforce were engaged in some form of information work by the turn of the 21st century." The fact that there are nearly 100 million information workers in the U.S. alone certainly suggests that we need to learn more about how we can evaluate efforts to help them work more productively; certainly, any broad-based improvements to information work could bring substantial benefits to the economy and society. Hence the focus on the information worker instead of the knowledge worker.

When she started thinking about information work productivity, Susan Conway says, "The first thought was to go out and engage some of the key economists to figure out how you modify current productivity measurements for measuring information work." It turned out not to be so easy.

Susan went looking for leading thinkers with enough interest in the subject that they would sign up to participate in the work of the Council. She described the Council as "a non-profit joint research effort by academic institutions, technology industry leaders, and technology consumers," and told people she talked to that she and the others involved in the effort were "tasked with the creation of a methodology, benchmark and business models to guide the business community toward opportunities that would improve information-work productivity."

Microsoft does not view the work of the Council as a company project, but instead as stepping up to the plate with funding and impetus to launch what the company hoped and expected would be a broadly based community effort involving businesses and academics. And that has certainly been happening. Formally launched in 2003, the Council now has a membership that includes Cisco, Accenture, HP, Intel, SAP, and Xerox; the academic institutions on the Council include schools of Harvard, MIT, NYU, UC Berkeley, and Babson College (in Wellsley, Massachusetts). Dozens of companies are having work processes examined by researchers associated with the Council.

During the initial research, it quickly became clear why no methods for measuring this kind of productivity have been widely accepted in the past. Information work is poorly defined and not visible in the production model currently used to measure productivity in the industrial economy. Susan explained, "You can't manage something you can't measure, but you can't measure something you can't identify. Identifying and quantifying are the components of information work." The effort is currently focused on gaining a better understanding of information work. The economists working with the Council will then address the problem of how to modify the current models of productivity, or build a new model, that includes information work.

No one involved is promising quick fixes or instant solutions.

Beyond ROI

The standard financial measures aren't the only yardsticks being used; some companies have been clever enough to see beyond what everyone else is doing. Washington Mutual CIO Jerry Gross—

> Return on investment of technology is a very good financial metric to try to shoot for, and we've done that. But we also have some non-financial or intangible metrics, and we believe that if you accomplish those, you can have tremendous success. One is employee enablement. In the technology that you're deploying, are employees becoming power users of that technology? Are they being fully empowered to utilize the technology?
>
> The people part is all about the behavioral. Whether the end user is an employee or the customer, do you see a behavioral change? Are they truly enabled? That's one important piece of it.

It may seem unexpected that the Army also needs to deal with ROI. The top technology boss, Lt. General Steven Boutelle, says that he sometimes has heard the question, "What's my return on investment in these networks and laptop computers and [secure] Dynamic Access devices?"

My answer consistently is 'survival.'

In business, if you are an early user, you have a short period of time that you will do business better than your competition—you'll probably get more contracts, and you'll have a better return on your investment, the margin will be better. But if you don't commit early, your competition will be bidding faster, they'll have information faster, they'll have information inside your decision cycle, and they will beat you consistently in doing business.

So in a perfect world, if all of the people in your industry adopt all these practices, you will not make any more money. But you will be in parity with your competition, and so you will survive and not go bankrupt.

You can almost draw that parallel into the military system. When the war fighter says, 'I don't want to spend money on a satellite dish and the distribution system for intelligence,' you can do that for a little while but pretty soon you're going to run up against the competition. We know even Al Queda uses the Internet, and they're going to be making decisions globally very quickly, faster than you do if you do not adopt these technologies to stay in parity. The power of America and our industry is to integrate those technologies better and faster than our adversaries or potential adversaries.

Return on investment may be an excellent measure of business value, but even in a perfect world we continually come face to face with the challenge of trying to determine the true ROI on a technology project. "Well, this is said every day and every week in every publication," Roger Smith commented. "It's so difficult to project what the return on investment is really going to be. You can only take so much time with the analysis because technology moves so fast. You spend a year analyzing the situation, and the opportunity may be gone when you make your decision. So it has to be a fairly quick process. We learn along the way."

Lawrence Baxter recalls that ROI and internal rate of return were subjects that suddenly become hot as a reaction to what was perceived to be a lot of wasted money in the dot-com world. But in his view, "I don't think companies always have processes in place to really enforce it." Wachovia does use the classic financial measures when evaluating major technology projects—

> I just had a project kicked out last week. It will come back and be approved at some point, but it got kicked out because it did-n't meet the required threshold of internal rate of return. And so we are getting much stricter about it than before. But processes can be gamed. Sometimes it is claimed that projects are 'infrastructural and don't have to show an internal rate of return.' But you know that can be a sort of special pleading and a means of avoiding the rigor of meeting a financial threshold.
>
> So I think finance managers seem to be showing much more rigor than ever before. You know we have to because one of the big skepticisms on the part of shareholders was whether a com-pany can actually control expenses. Perhaps this is unique to us—at least our people keep telling us other companies aren't imposing the same constraints. And I keep saying, 'I bet they are.' Maybe we are just a little more sensitive to it than some other companies because Wall Street is watching us so closely.

In fact, the question isn't whether your company uses financial measures; all companies do. The question is whether your company uses financial measures to predict and track technology projects, and whether the processes are in place to cancel a project in trou-ble on a timely basis.

Applying Technology to a Busted Process

It may be obvious and seem like stomping over too-familiar ground, but many a problem owes its cause to applying new technology with-out first examining the underlying business processes. Tyson Foods' Steve Hankins has learned by experience—

> I think what people really need to understand is how technol-ogy fits into the business. Sometimes it's the tendency on the part of IT management, especially from the old school of 'data processing' people, to say, 'We'll give you a program, it'll do what you need,' without fully understanding that the technol-ogy is supposed to be an enabler of the business process.

If the business process is broken at the outset, technology can't help. Even great technology won't fix a bad process. It actually makes the situation worse. Paving over the cow path really doesn't do you any good.

So you can't think about change in your technology infrastructure separately from business process improvement, or even reengineering. Converting an organization to think in terms of business processes and the process steps and the enabling technology and such is a challenge.

Justifying a Technology Spend at Airborne

In the previous chapter we described a technology project at Airborne that allowed customers easy access to package tracking information without having to phone the company's call center. Of course there's a financial side to that story, as well. Rachelle Mileur explained—

> We were trying to come up with ways that we could try out .Net technology to see if it provided as much productivity as touted. But we wanted to try it on a project that would deliver business value at the same time. And from a business perspective, you can't do that unless you deliver immediate value.

Once the team had selected the tracking information project, they approached the business unit with the idea—

> The process of getting this project off the ground began with piquing the business side's interest. They said, 'Great, but how much will it cost?'

By moving the process from "should we" to "how can we," Rachelle and the rest of her team had managed to get the response they wanted. It meant the business unit was interested—

> Now it's up to IT to come back to them and say how much it will cost and how long it will take. Then the business people have to justify and quantify the benefits that will offset these costs to the extent that we can generate a positive return.
>
> If a positive return is viable then we take it to an executive committee and say 'IT believes it will cost this much and take this long, and the business side believes it will return these kinds of benefits.' From there, it's up to the business to decide

relative to the other priorities if this project will go forward or not. And they did.

IT is able to work with the business partners in estimating the cost of developing a new technology because it's much more of a known, and easy to quantify. Coming up with reasonable numbers in this case was easy for us to determine, because we knew how much a call cost us. We can project if we had X number of fewer calls, we would be able to save Y amount of dollars.

The other benefit that this solution had was that it would only require about ten weeks of development in addition to having a very low cost of entry. So the hurdle to get over in terms of proving business benefits was lower.

In the end, the business side was pleased because the project was not only proving the new technology, but offered the possibility of a customer benefit at the same time—

We were implementing a concept of an incremental building system that gives results through continually delivering small chunks of functionality, rather than the old fashioned approach that can take long periods of time to develop an entire system at once.

This was our first foray into changing our approach by installing one solution that we have developed, and then integrating several additional concepts as they roll off the line.

The project actually came in a little under budget. And we are tracking the usage of it and then correlating that to tracking call volume, to prove the return on investment.

Technology Spending Decisions and ROI in the Small Company

As the interviews in this book demonstrate, in large organizations the failure to be absolutely certain that there was a payoff should reside not with the technology people but with the business people. Terry Szpak of Telesystems West has his own explanation—and it's not one that IT folks will take as a compliment: "The technology people, they just want all the toys. Whereas the business people are so much more objective."

In some cases the smaller company has the advantage because the top management is so much closer to the business than management at a big firm can be. Terry said, "I just know if I have to spend a lot of money for something, I want to make sure it's worth it for me."

That's the other aspect—in a small business, each of these decisions is a big deal. A couple of wrong ones, and suddenly the company may not be in business. So in a small company, the motivation to stay close enough that you have a feel for whether the technology dollars are paying off comes from a strong survival instinct. But in the end, as with just about everything else in life, it comes down to a matter of priorities and choices.

Eric Meslow, the founder and CEO of Timbercon, a $5 million a year fiber optic manufacturer in Oregon, offered this perspective—

The problem for us is that all those priorities can be difficult to gauge. How do you put a dollar value on keeping your purchasing manager from tearing his hair out because he's using archaic, limited hardware and software? How do you put a dollar value on making your accountant much happier because she's that much more organized? These are very difficult decisions, but even without being able to run ROI and getting an answer that provides clarity and business sense, I know these are investments that have to be made and we'll just have to bite the bullet.

We are currently allocating quite a bit of revenue to high-tech improvements. Number one is backbone infrastructure. We have reached a size where we can no longer run off of one small server and continue to ignore data back up or redundancy. Our exposure for catastrophic failure is too great, and unplanned downtime is too expensive. To that end, we've been investing a significant amount of money in our IT infrastructure to alleviate the danger.

But that's nothing compared to the broader decision of evaluating and moving to a new MRP and accounting customer/service software package. We're looking at mid-market packages that run from $60,000 to about $120,000, with anywhere from 15 to 17 percent annual recurring licensing fees.

Eric then described the impact of that expenditure in a way that surely hits home with everyone who has ever held a key position in a small business:

The moment I pull the trigger on this purchase, that's two employees I can't hire. That is a huge investment for us.

When you come right down to it, some infrastructure decisions are in a class with deciding whether you need a telephone. But is it all gut instinct, or are there times when even small business leaders apply financial measurements? Eric again:

I've done Return on Investment work in regard to programs like AutoCAD and SolidWorks [a program for designing mechanical components], and some of the other engineering tools we've purchased. When a need is being driven by a particular project, you know how much revenue you've got coming in, you know how much the software product costs, you know how much you're going to use it. You can analyze the numbers and say, 'Okay this thing will pay for itself in the first six months.' That's a no-brainer.

And then you have something like a $100,000 accounting software decision. How much would we save? We could see $5,000 here, $2,000 there, $5,000 someplace else, and it added up to $17,000 a year, which takes five years to break even. Add to that the recurring license fees, about $15,000 a year, and for us, it never pays off.

But these numbers are at our current level. If we double or triple our size, it's going to be a different story. What we're about to face is what many companies face when they emerge out of one or two million dollars in annual sales, and start breaking into the tens of millions. A culture change occurs once you reach a certain level in size, and technology requirements become exponentially more expensive. When I think about the investment and work that level of growth is going require, it makes me wish we were already beyond it.

Meslow looks at the arithmetic he faces and finds it frustrating—

Currently we use a software accounting package that costs around $2,000 to purchase, that has no recurring upgrade costs or licensing fees, and gets 85 percent to 90 percent of our job done. When our growth requires that we step up to the next level, that remaining 10 to 15 percent is going to cost us up to $100,000. That, coupled with up to a $15,000 a year fee to keep it licensed, all in the hope to approach 100 percent functionality.

That's frustrating for me as an owner because that is an exorbitant expense for little improvement in performance. By comparison, I wouldn't give an employee $100,000 raise for 15 percent more output.

In the end, the only way a small company can justify this type of expense is by believing that, ultimately, their staff of twenty-five people will become a staff of 250. The transition is difficult, one of those challenging business decisions for which an investment is part of the calculation. But other factors weigh strongly as well—

> The big thing is timing the decision in such a way that the cost doesn't kill you. We can afford to make that $100,000 investment; and if it was wrong, it's not going to put us out of business. But combine that with losing a large customer—or some other type of setback—then we're out of business.
>
> We have always tried to limit our exposure to these kinds of situations. With this particular case, we're taking a bit of a gamble.

But right now, Eric acknowledges, they are, technologically, "extremely happy." He explains, "Everybody's on the same version of the operating system, everybody's on the same version of Office, everybody's on the same Exchange server."

As for the challenge he confronts over the software expenditure, "It's a huge burden because it's all upfront money. It just a big hurdle that a growing company of our size faces. If we were able to forecast a sales increase of $2 million due to technology investments this wouldn't be a big deal at all. We do not see that type of return at this point; the hope is that over several years it will continue to help us grow"

To which I replied, "This will be a motivator to get there that much quicker."

Eric answered, "There you are, there you are—we gotta go close some business."

Take-Aways

Few people who have thoughtfully considered the question would disagree with the idea that the business case for a technology project should belong to the business side, not to IT. It's long past time that this issue was put to rest and no longer debated. But still today, getting business unit leaders to step up to the plate often proves more difficult than it's supposed to be.

A major element of the answer calls for making the leader of the business unit take ownership of any major technology project being done for him. He'll do this in partnership with IT, of course, but let's not have any further debate about who the owner of the project should be. This 'commandment' was one of the most important messages from the people who shared ideas for this book, and is one of the most important take-aways.

What's more, the business leader has to know that he is going to be held accountable for the success of the project. And having taken ownership, he needs to make sure the effort is viewed as a business project, not a technology project.

Virtually everyone interviewed for this book agreed that no major technology project should be started without a thorough benefits analysis. But beyond that, every manager in the company needs to be on the same page about this. There needs to be a single method everyone uses for the cost/benefit analysis or pre-implementation study. The company needs to pick one approach—whether it's ROI or net present value or any one of the other standard methods—and insist everyone use that method and not, as in some companies, "each one rolls his own." Personally, my own term for this is "defining success up front."

Making the business case for a company's technology expenditures is far too important to take for granted. Heads-up companies keep in touch with research and new developments. The new Information Worker Productivity Council will become a valuable source for keeping companies abreast of the subject.

Problems frequently occur when a company adapts new technology without first examining the underlying business processes. Overlaying good (and expensive) technology atop out of date, clumsy, or inappropriate business practices pretty much guarantees lots of unhappy internal customers. Examining and, if necessary, remaking business processes always needs to be a first step for any large-scale technology project.

Okay—so your company now requires developing and presenting a business case before a major technology investment is approved, and makes the business leader take ownership of the project and be accountable for it. Fine. But once the new technology is up and running, what are you doing to determine whether the benefits promised going in are in fact being realized?

That's the subject of the next chapter.

5

Making the Business Case for Technology, II: Demonstrating Value After the Fact

> [Having an external auditing group] is both good and bad. When you have people devoted to finding stuff, they find stuff. And once they find it, then you've got to fix it.
>
> — Stan Hupfeld, *CEO, Integris Health*

While many companies devote significant effort to the upfront analysis of technology projects, most give only token attention to any sort of after-the-fact evaluation. No single issue raised in this book holds greater potential for assuring that your organization will derive appropriate business value from its technology dollars than the issue that is the main focus of this chapter: conducting a routine and vigorous after-the-fact cost/benefit analysis on every major technology project.

If you were to recommend reading just one chapter of this book to a friend, your boss, or your CEO, I would want it to be this chapter.

Of course, the subject isn't exactly new. As mentioned earlier, I honestly don't remember a time in my career where there wasn't some focus on the idea of looking at the promised benefits of a technology project to determine if those benefits were actually achieved. Nonetheless, this remains a topic of discussion because the simple truth is that most companies are still not doing much about holding someone's feet to the fire on achieving benefits from technology.

By far the largest percentage of companies, when pushed, say that they do not do a disciplined job of auditing after a project has been installed. They don't verify whether or not the goals were met. Many seem to believe that achieving the benefits promised frankly would demand significant changes in the way the business is run—moving people around, possibly changing processes that have been in place for a lot of years, possibly laying people off. Many companies say they 'sort of' do an audit, when what they really mean is that in the end, they don't. And so these people are left scratching their heads—'Hey, I spent all this money, did it really pay for itself?'

The intentions may be good but too often the follow-through simply doesn't happen. We begin by looking at companies where audits are not yet the name of the game.

Resistance

At Mary Kay, CIO Kregg Jodie recognizes the company could be gaining value by taking that backward look to evaluate its technology decisions. But his IT department is not doing that on a consistent basis. What would it take for them to get to the point where he would say, "Okay, we're going to begin doing this?"

> I think you need to raise the level of awareness enough that people say, 'Oh, yeah, you're right, this is something that we need to take the time to do on a consistent basis.' People need to be aware we are not meeting our fiduciary responsibilities when we allow projects to get done without fully examining if we met the initial business objectives we set out to meet.

Kregg puts the responsibility on the IT leaders. "If we raise that issue and then standardize a process to evaluate the success or failure of our initiatives, we can do a better job at post-project assessments." But what's holding people up? Integris Health CEO Stan Hupfeld thinks that looking back shouldn't be necessary—

> You go through the process, you acquire new technology, you see what's going to work, you debug it and try to fix it. But you don't necessarily go back and compare the business case, the one you made originally, to how it really turned out. We've all seen so many changes in how we interact with technology, you almost think it's a crime to question it. Maybe there's just some blind faith involved.

Kregg Jodie doesn't agree—

As with many things, it's more of a journey than a destination, and we're making progress. Historically, I believe that the IT group did not give the business functions enough information to help with analysis in a timely fashion. Over the last five or six years, we've begun to provide more and more of that information via our data warehouse and other toolsets. Our business areas are eager to gain knowledge and review the performance of all our system initiatives—they just needed the tools, and education on how to use them.

From here on, as we implement projects we'll be focused on what the system is going to do in terms of increased revenue, labor efficiencies, decreased cost, stronger relationships with clients, competitive advantage, and so on.

Kregg cautions, however, that an after-the-fact analysis can be clouded by a variety of factors—

Once you've already determined how you will measure the success of the project, then you just need to audit that at predetermined points of time. Some metrics are difficult to measure—for example, increased revenue could have resulted from many different initiatives, or could be the result of pulling sales forward from one month to another. However, despite these challenges, we're making an effort to track the different variables.

I don't see any reason why we as IT professionals couldn't say up front, 'Here's how I've defined the value of this, and here is what I'm expecting that we'll get out of it.' And then, maybe as milestones built throughout the plan, we would figure to come back at predetermined points of time—maybe it's 25 percent of implementation complete, 50 percent, and so on. Or maybe there are other natural milestones that fall out of the project plan. But we should be able to come back at those predetermined points of time to say not only how are we relative to the timeline we established for this particular project, but how are we relative to the value and delivering the value that we have expected to deliver.

So Kregg is figuring out on his own what I've been calling for all along. But Craig Cuyar acknowledges that the situation at Common-Health with regard to after-the-fact analysis is unchanged, which he says is much the same as at other places he has worked—

I can tell you from my personal and professional experiences, which include other organizations besides CommonHealth: the answer is 'No'—we aren't doing formal financial reviews after a project has been completed. I'll just be very bold and frank about this. We talk a good deal about business value and project justification as 'up front' analyses, but do very little, if any, financial analyses after the project has been implemented

I say 'investment decision' because ultimately all of these decisions should be viewed as an investment. As CIO's, we are charged with the responsibility of making decisions about where to invest our company's money. These 'investment decisions' have a present and future value that should be carefully considered when assessing which projects will provide the most business value to an organization.

To me, that's a brilliant way to look at a technology spend: not as a cost but as an investment.

I've got a finite amount of capital—how do I invest that at the greatest return? It may be a technology initiative; it may be just putting it in the bank or riding the stock market.

In any case, when it comes to making investment decisions, we have all the upfront analyses and we can predict the payback period, internal rate of return, the net present value, the reduced head count, the incremental revenue gain, and so on. But I have never had audits after a project where someone has come back to say, 'Craig, you promised X number of reductions in this group of employees and you've actually hired two more people.' Or, 'You committed to have a payback period of 12 months and it's now 13 months and I'm only 75 percent completed with the project.' It doesn't happen.

If we really want to talk about the value of an IT investment and how we could make that valuation process better or more effective, I think we don't necessarily need to spend any more time with the upfront analysis because I think most organizations today are spending the appropriate amount of due diligence in that decision-making process.

But I think we could really provide greater value by being able to have audits at predetermined points in time to make sure that we're actually delivering against what we planned as a result of the 'up front' analyses.

In our interview with Craig, I shared with him—as I did with others when talking about this subject—that I actually think it's financially irresponsible not to do audits after a major project. A company spends all that time up front, and then in the end the percentage of projects that are audited, I'm going to guess, would be a single-digit percentage.

GMAC-RFC's Rick Greenwood has his own explanation of why this isn't being done: "I think a lot of times what happens is that these are multi-million dollar projects, but the discipline is not in place to ask the questions about, 'What actually changed in the environment? Was the value actually achieved?'" Still, he says, the effort isn't being ignored. "We're not 100 percent there, but we've made very, very good progress on it. And that really helps."

Other companies recognize the need, but are taking small steps. Typical is Wachovia, as explained by Lawrence Baxter:

> I don't think [after-the-fact analysis is] disciplined yet. We have a rule that a 10 percent variance from the initial projection requires a return visit to the financial review committee. And so there's an effort to track it. But 10 percent is a very sloppy term because the notion of a project being on budget is very dependent on whether it's on time. A project that's running late is by definition not on budget because of the time that's being burned up.
>
> The level of rigor in tracking is still probably not very rigorous. We're all still learning how.
>
> So, yes, a full scale audit is really the only way, and it would have to be an audit of actual and opportunity dollars. And you know there are number of reasons that this kind of accounting gets buried in the dust of the follow up after the initial implementation.

Rick reassures himself by adding a note of scepticism: "I doubt whether anyone is yet at that stage."

CommonHealth turned out to be one company that isn't doing after-the-fact evaluations, yet is still far enough along in their thinking to picture how it might work. Craig Cuyar recognizes the shared burden for achieving value, and the role of the business unit, as discussed earlier. He envisions how this might work—

> At CommonHealth, we would take the lead within our IT organization to push out. And we would say, 'We plan to be

held accountable for delivering X or Y value. And to the extent that you can help us deliver that value, we can provide additional funding for your projects.' Or, 'We could fund this project because we recognize it's a joint effort between the IT organization and the local business unit to deliver that value.'

We would need people to understand that it's not on IT's shoulders to deliver that value, because we can't do it without the business unit. And it's not solely the responsibility of the business unit to deliver value because they can't do it without the IT organization.

Here Craig was joining the argument in favor of joint ownership. If the onus is on IT alone for having to stand up for the cost/benefit analysis, then you fail to achieve the sense of responsibility that comes from making this a two-way street—

You lose the sense of focus, you lose the responsibility. But I would say more importantly, with responsibility comes accountability. As the representative of the IT organization, I don't want to be held accountable for revenue numbers or head count numbers within an individual business unit. And that's where I think it really needs to be a shared responsibility.

I believe in the end, if you're unwilling or unable to take on this responsibility, then you have almost no right to criticize. Craig joins in this view, and takes it a step further, challenging my opinion—

You keep using the word 'responsibility,' and I view it not as a responsibility; it's *accountability*. The CIO can deliver the best value to his or her organization by being accountable for not only demonstrating business value, but also for actually delivering it.

Moving in the Right Direction

Meanwhile, other companies are further along in adopting an after-the-fact audit process. But an effective process that holds people accountable has to have strong buy-in across the board—because there are some risks. The leading risk is the most obvious one: it may show your project was a failure. So gearing up for putting an audit process in place needs to include making sure people become comfortable with the process, and comfortable with the possibility that it can show that their projects aren't living up to the promises.

How you roll out the process, how aggressively you implement it, needs to reflect the culture of the organization.

An on-going effort at Lloyds bank has involved a series of about forty efficiency and productivity improvement efforts within an overall business transformation. At the same time, Archie Kane explained, Lloyds was putting an audit process into place—

> The program was run by a rod of iron. We on the steering committee were constantly going around following up with our people. We were saying, 'All right, where are the benefits,' and, 'I'm sorry but I don't buy this—that isn't an auditable benefit, I want an auditable benefit.'
>
> So it was pretty in-your-face, and that's why some people didn't like it. We knew exactly what we spent on those projects, and we know exactly the benefits that we got out of them in terms of head-count removed, or in terms of cost savings or business gains.
>
> We haven't got that [follow-up] across all of the other projects that we do in the bank. But on that series of projects we spent about 500 million pounds over a period of three and a half years, and we've gained benefits of about 400 million per annum in annualized benefits.
>
> That is all audited. We used a very strict discipline on it.

The specific accounting method is not the major issue; that will vary from one company to another. More important to ponder is what the senior management will consider valuable. From his experience at CommonHealth, Craig Cuyar suggested where he thinks the emphasis belongs: "A lot of organizations are using discounted cash flow models based upon NPV [net present value] to determine the benefit of project A relative to project B. What that can do is to make people become a little more conservative with upfront analyses. If they know they're going to be held accountable at the end, they're going to make sure those numbers are accurate."

He went on to add, "I've seen a number of organizations that apply very liberal 'assumptions' while calculating the business value of particular projects just to have them funded. In these organizations, the combination of liberal assumptions and no true accountability afford the opportunity to fund projects that may ultimately never deliver the promised returns."

At Lloyds, some business leaders in the bank, Archie Kane reports, were not happy with his trying to insist on applying this kind of audit discipline to some of their projects. But it takes consistency and a firm hand; whatever methodology is used, it needs to be applied uniformly across the organization. Otherwise you dilute the value, because the numbers mean different things in different organizations. Archie explained, "Business management is happy with the result of that project, but I have to say the reaction is mixed. We had a pretty hardnosed discipline that if you took the money, you had to deliver the benefits. People tend to not always respond well to that. You know, there's a great deal of, 'I need the investment to drive my business,' with the benefits getting lost in the mist."

The problems can be exaggerated when senior business managers are not as comfortable with technology as they should be, Archie insists—

We've got a particular program that we've been working on now for eighteen months that we've just decided to slow down. And the reason why? Because the business guys don't want to have to face up to the hard decisions. The IT guys have been pushing this like crazy.

If I was running that side of the business, I'd be in there pulling this thing as hard and fast as I could, because it's the future of that business. I'd see it as the platform that's going to allow me to compete in the future and to develop, to be more flexible, and so on.

But they [the business side] don't always feel that way. And it's difficult—it's changing the habits of a lifetime, and it's facing up to such things as 'I'm going to have to retrain all my people, I'm going to have to communicate with my customers, I'm going to have to do this now.'

Well, if you are not doing it, your competitors sure as hell are out there doing it. So to me, the big defining limit now is the ability of the business to change rapidly and to reinvent itself and to retrain itself for those customers. That's the defining factor at the moment.

As mentioned elsewhere in the book, some companies forestall interfering with a project, only to discover when it's done that it hasn't met expectations. ChevronTexaco avoids that with a process Dave Clementz calls "the look-back":

We have so many checkpoints along the way where we can see if a project is sliding sideways. We have a five-step process that we use for all major projects. And in each major phase of the project there's a gate you have to get through. At that gate, you have a Decision Review Board, which for major projects is our CIO Council. And you have a decision executive; again, for major projects, that would usually be the CIO himself. And if you can't get past this gateway, then you figure out how to solve it or the project doesn't go. We can stop the project and get a recycle or we can just shut it down. And that prevents you from getting all the way to the Executive Committee and having to tell them you have a failure.

Roger Smith laughed when he described the progress of technology governance at Marsh—

We've come a long way. Five years ago a business leader would say, 'Give this to me and I'll make millions.' And when it was done, we'd say, 'This process should have reduced staff; where are they?'

'Oh, they're still here, they're doing something else.'

And it becomes this paper chase. 'Okay, what are they doing?' 'Oh, they're doing this over here and that over there.' We are growing every year, so the staff translation might not have been the right measure. But we couldn't always pin down the savings that enabling a process with technology was supposed to have delivered.

Now we're saying, 'Show me the picture today, show me the picture in three years, where does the shift occur?' Ask business leaders to project out two to three years, and then work backwards. That's a pretty good exercise.

Roger has had plenty of opportunity to learn some tricks about managing the IT aspects of an operation. In the late 1980's, his division had 10,000 people; through acquisitions and growth, it now has over 38,000. Echoing the famous remark by the late Senator Everett Dirksen, Roger comments that "When you add up a spend here and a spend there, all of a sudden you're talking about some real money."

In the process, Marsh has become much more earnest about verifying the benefits of IT expenditures—

I'd say there are three reasons that has happened, and I think it's all called 'learning as we go.' One, we had a major technology investment a number of years ago in a system that just never happened. I'm sure there are parallels in a lot of major companies, where you spend millions of dollars on something, it gets bigger and bigger and bigger, and then it never gets fully delivered. Software and a lot of development time, and a lot of feature creep, and it was just never ending. We had to modify the overall project and shelve some of the technology.

The big lesson learned here is the effect of buying off-the-shelf solutions. I think that, up to this project, we had a bias toward build and we spent a lot of money on this build. Like many large companies, we have unique operations and may require unique technology solutions. But we now have a much better filter through which to evaluate buy vs. build.

Secondly, would we be spending money but not delivering hard cost improvement in [the] top line or bottom line? In one situation where we'd spent money, we went back to the business a year later and said, 'Okay, what did this do for you?'

They said, 'Thanks, it's super, works great—now we can get paperclips in three days instead of five.'

We said, 'The bank spent X dollars so you could do that.'

'Oh!'

So sometimes there were just incredible disconnects between the amount we spent and the return. It was not because we hadn't really thought about it. I don't think anyone was prepared for how ubiquitous technology became in the 1990's. For example, six years ago our U.S. offices were not all connected through a network. Today, we feel a twinge if a database takes more than five seconds to load. And with 38,000 users, think about the implication of migrating from a newer version of the operating system. Pick any price point per seat, and do the math—it's an attention-getter.

So we encountered a typical technology Catch 22—having spent the technology dollars for one of our business segments on systems they did not highly value, but that used up most of their technology budget for the fiscal year, with the remaining amount needed for infrastructure, and nothing left for new applications.

Clearly, no way to run technology. And this brought us to a more thoughtful and diligent process.

The Audit Process in Action

In the late 1980's, Tyson Foods acquired several large companies, and Steve Hankins became the team leader of seeing to the integration of the new businesses into the parent company, which he says gave him the opportunity to understand how every facet of the company worked.

In 1989, when revenues were approaching $2 billion, the company made a decision to do what Steve Hankins refers to as "throwing out the mainframe." But then Tyson bought Holly Farms, which was also a $2 billion company. In the process of trying to put the two firms together, the throw-out-the-mainframe project got sidetracked. Steve Hankins explained, "At that time the CFO called me in and said, 'Since you're the biggest griper, I want you to go run the computer department.'" It was an early example of what later became a habit: send someone into the fray who doesn't have a history in the old computer world.

With the mainframe project now in his hands, Steve went ahead with the original intention of getting rid of their ancient Sperry Rand—

> I threw it out. Threw it out, set it on the sidewalk, and let the rain fall on it.
>
> But the computer itself was not a problem. The problem was the mentality of the people running the IS department. When I came to work at Tyson, part of my deal was I had to have a PC. And so I actually bought and brought in the first personal computer that we used at Tyson Foods; I still have my disks from Lotus 123 version 1A.
>
> After we got rid of the mainframe, I found faster, better, cheaper ways of doing a lot of things, especially as it related to our accounting work.

In his early days running IT, "There were so many projects that we did just simply because if you're going to throw out the mainframe, you find a lot of things you need to replace." They were so busy that "We didn't much focus on doing audits." That began to change as the dust settled. "As we started moving on to projects that weren't part of the old portfolio, then we began to do reviews of what the results had been. And so, for instance, we implemented a transportation system and did a lot of things around that, and we did reviews of those for quite a while, until people were so con-vinced that this was an overwhelming winner that we didn't have those questions anymore." To which he added the observation that "it's not always a formalized process."

While Integris Health has not reached the level of commitment to auditing that CEO Stan Hupfeld would like, they nonetheless have an active program—

> As to doing an evaluation of whether we got the benefit of some new technology—no, so far that has not been a focus. I think that's the next level. First we need to do all the kind of baseline stuff—insuring security, insuring that everybody's in compliance with password turnover, insuring that all the vendors are meeting their requirements, and those kind if things.
>
> Once we do all that, then the next step is to move our audi-tors into the phase of 'Are we getting all the bang for the buck out of the technology that we've acquired?' And against the pro forma that we first did on a project, both financial and operational, has it really met those expectations?
>
> We currently go back and audit a fairly minor percentage of our IT investments. But we have a very aggressive audit func-tion. Our internal audit department has five auditors devoted entirely to IT.
>
> Of course, that's both good and bad. When you have people devoted to finding stuff, they find stuff. And once they find it, then you've got to fix it. We're reasonably new at this, but the IT auditors are very good, and you know, some of it is as picayune as door locks and those kinds of things, security issues. A lot of it has to do with contracts, and if the vendors live up to their obligations. A lot of it has to do with our own internal security issues.

A number of the people we spoke with, while agreeing that vali-dation should be done, believed it could be worthwhile only if it were done at arm's length—meaning by people outside the man-agement of the group that the project was being done for.

At one extreme was the view that you should have a separate group, whose sole job would be something on the order of a military Inspector General, evaluating whether technology projects came through with the promised benefits and accountable directly to the top. Among those holding this view was Lloyds' Archie Kane—

We're going to have a function that will report on the progress of the major projects to the group executive committee, taking a slightly independent view. A thing like that in the past would have been hard to do, but we're probably going to expand this group's role. But I have to say, it remains to be seen how strong this idea is and what kind of teeth it will have.

As we move into this different way of operating, there's going to be an increase in accountability and less room for excuses.

At the time we spoke, Lloyds had only had one experience with using the separate functional oversight group, and had seen mixed reactions. Even so, senior management appeared to be even more committed to that approach—

The direction we're going in is much more business-units based. I hate using the 'e-word' because I think it's used and abused—people think 'empowerment' means 'Just give me a budget and let me run off and do what I want, and never hold me accountable.' Empowerment doesn't mean anything unless it's in a clear framework and comes with clear accountability.

So I believe there must be a kind of high-level framework in which the business units decide what IT projects they want to spend money on and how much they're going to spend. But they are then held accountable for delivery of the results. No excuses, you can't turn around and blame IT, you can't turn around and blame some service providers, be they internal or external. It's your job to solve on your own.

Archie added, "It's going to be interesting to see how that manifests itself."

The Challenge of Audits in a Small Company

In a small company, it may be difficult for the owners to see a benefit in spending time on proving the value of a technology investment. The thinking ones recognize the potential even if they have trouble paying attention to the issue, given the pressures of everything else going on.

Asked if his company goes to the trouble of auditing the business value of technology expenditures, Telesystems West founder Terry Szpak said, "I just don't have the time right now because of a large project we're working on that keeps me traveling. But I know just from some of the sales in the last few months that we make the numbers easily every month to justify our latest expenditure."

How does a company draw the line between going to the trouble to audit versus senior management just being close enough in touch to know whether something is working? Do they leave at the end of the day troubled about whether or not there has been a payoff? Do they bring in help to give them a sure answer? Terry Szpak: "There's no way I would pay a third-party company to come in to see if I'm making money doing that because I have a good feel at the bottom line of how we're doing. I can see the sales come in, I'm speaking directly to the customers who are buying." But he recognized the small-company advantage: "If we were a large corporation, I wouldn't have that feel."

A Model Program at Washington Mutual

One fundamental principle overrides every other in this effort: being consistent in demanding that all significant technology projects be audited. Consistency is key. The effort at Washington Mutual seems to have this notion as a guidepost, as CIO Jerry Gross explained—

> We've got a program in place where there's a very strict standardized template that needs to be completed for every single project over a certain dollar amount that has a business case associated with it. The template goes into not only the financial business case, but how this project ties back to the strategic seams of the company for that year, what specific goals and objectives it's driving toward, and so forth. And a lot of projects don't make it past that point.
>
> Those that do then go in front of the CapEx [Capital Expenditures Committee]. Once the project is completed, we go back and review. We don't review every single project, but we'll have a list of those that met their business case and those that didn't. And for those that didn't, what were the extenuating circumstances?
>
> You've got to have tremendous discipline to review the results of projects once they've hit some milestones. One of the things that we gain from this CapEx process, as well as the quarterly business reviews, is a clearer view of how certain project managers and project teams are several times more suc-

cessful than others. I like to say past results are an indicator of future attempts. It's the antithesis of that disclaimer you get when you're looking at mutual funds.

We have a unique way of doing this. Most companies snapshot where their key projects are as of right now with red, yellow, or green coding. We have project trending that goes on over time; we continue to capture the color coding. We start to see trends; if some project teams always end up red, then there's something systemic going on.

So once again, it's looking at how we achieve process excellence in execution and deployment of projects. And the life cycle doesn't end once you've deployed it. The maintenance and support is also an issue, whether you ultimately outsource it or put it into some sort of maintenance program.

But we go back and take a look at the business case for every project that gets to see the light of day.

In short, to hold business leaders accountable, the organization needs to create an objective, respected process. An independent audit team or organization should be established, to do a follow-up audit on every significant technology project, determining whether the promised business goals were realized.

The lack of holding people accountable is the biggest source of failure and waste on technology projects.

Validating with User Surveys

As well as having some clever approaches to tracking projects, Washington Mutual also has been following what I consider a novel approach to auditing. As CIO Jerry Gross explained, it involves user surveys: "We focus on employee enablement and customer satisfaction. We have a series of surveys that are done with the employee community. For example, annually we have an all-employee survey that doesn't ask people, 'Did you think this project had a good return on investment?' It's more along the lines of, 'Do you feel more enabled with the new desktop software?' And one item may say, 'Please rank the ways your role has changed.'

"We also do other surveys quarterly. From these we can then deduce which of the implementations we did were of real value.

"This is better than anecdotal, even though it's not the dollars and cents stuff that the CFO will ultimately look at it. However,"

Jerry insisted," these feedback words can be very convincing. It's very hard to argue against that."

Take-Aways

We cannot continue to criticize whether technology has truly paid off unless we are willing to step up to the responsibility of conducting follow-up audits as a standard practice, a requirement. You have no business criticizing technology for not fulfilling its promise or potential unless you have a formal process in place for determining what benefit was actually realized from each technology project.

While it appears that not many companies are where they want to be in this regard—if they have even started at all—there is at least a consensus that it is indeed an issue that needs to be addressed.

But these audits need to look at more than whether new technology performs to the level it is supposed to. They also need to look at how well the change management process was handled.

An audit may suggest that what you got was primarily productivity gain that allows you to do more efficiently what you were already doing. In that case you then need to go the next step, asking yourself, "If that's true, what is being done with the time that has been freed up?"

How about infrastructure projects—does an audit even make sense? The answer is that an audit is equally important, even if it goes no further than comparing the actual cost against the original estimate.

To repeat a point made earlier, the whole issue turns on a core business principle of accountability. For every technology project with expected business value, you need to be naming the person who will be accountable, and then requiring them to demonstrate whether the investment made sense when measured against the promises.

If you were to become convinced and passionate about just one issue presented in this book, I would want it to be the core idea of this chapter—that performing an analysis after the fact to determine whether the benefits promised had actually been achieved needs to be a routine practice in every organization—even in a company where the IT "staff" consists of just a single person.

PART THREE

Governance, Culture, and the Challenge of Running IT

6

Let's Give Governance a Chance

We prefer to populate oversight groups with colleagues who have revenue responsibility...A staff person who doesn't speak our professionals' language gets less respect.

—Rick Greenwood, *GMAC-RFC*

"Governance." In this context, it means the role of the people or group who oversee technology projects. And it also means the agreed-upon way that IT and the business side are going to jointly shoulder the task of implementing technology and measuring benefits. Just about every business leader and entrepreneur I've talked to in recent years agrees that governance should not be ignored. And while the effort is by no means universal, many companies have an operation already in place and have valuable insights to share, while many others without a program are making an effort to get one started.

Getting Started with Governance

Tyson Foods' CFO Steve Hankins agrees that the idea of governance is catching on. "A few years ago," he says, "I was more hands on, but for anything that was significant and new, there was a collaborative discussion with the senior management team. We didn't call it a steering committee, but in fact they functioned like one." Today, he says, that has changed. "We now have a formal [governance] committee."

But getting started with governance is not without its challenges, as GMAC-RFC's Rick Greenwood found out—

The governance structure we put in place is made up of our senior management team—the senior executive vice presidents of each of our six businesses within the Residential Capital Group, plus myself, and our group CFO It's a joint governance between the business group and IT.

We have a process, kind of a portfolio management process. The business unit people fill out the paperwork, and we go through that. The group meets on a semiannual basis, but then there are other people who get together on a quarterly basis, as well.

We've spent a lot of time on this value proposition. The six businesses leverage one another, and we talk about the portfolio effect of leveraging each of the businesses. So when a project comes forward, it might be that this project may benefit two or three business units and they will understand the magnitude of that. And IT and finance are brought in to supply the appropriate services and capabilities to make it happen.

It's worked out really well for us but, you know, it's been a struggle. I'm not saying it's an easy thing to do, but it's definitely been the right thing to do.

Who should sit on a governance council? At Marsh, they have strong views on the subject. "We prefer to populate these oversight groups with colleagues who have revenue responsibility," Roger Smith told us. "If someone is heading up a division but also has a responsibility for governance, he or she takes a different view of the priorities. People in our companies tend to respect people in revenue producing positions more than some staff people. A staff person who doesn't speak our professionals' language gets less respect."

Another challenge: It can be difficult for members of a governance council to take a broad view instead of being partial to the needs of their own business segment. Roger described it this way:

[At Marsh,] we have a lot of verbiage in our senior leaders' guidelines to say one of your jobs is to act in the best interest of the firm. A senior leader in a U.S. business segment may be called upon to think independently of the needs of his or her segment think in terms of the overall corporate needs.

So one when one segment says, 'We absolutely, positively have to have this, and it's going to cost X million,' while another department says, 'We need this other thing, and it also has a big price tag.' Someone has to make a decision of which comes first, do we do both, can we draft one off the other. That has to take place at a pretty high level.

As we've seen in earlier chapters, even with a formal governance process, you still need continuing oversight while a project is underway. Lawrence Baxter explained the signposts at Wachovia Bank: "We try to size projects at an early stage in order to stop them from going too far in terms of company commitment of expenditure on a project we don't know enough about." But then there are those projects that, even with oversight, don't work out as anticipated. "Sometimes," Baxter said, "you take on a project that turns out to be much more difficult than you ever imagined or that anybody in the industry might have imagined. Sometimes I look back at a project and think, 'We were in such a fog of the unknown that it's a miracle we actually got it done on budget and on time.'"

Airborne is another company that has learned the lesson of erecting quick barriers on projects that aren't working out. Rachelle Mileur explained—

> Traditionally at Airborne, projects have been delivered as a system at a time. It's a sign of the times in today's economic climate that I'm less willing to risk a large amount of capital in hopes that these projected benefits are true.
>
> The best IT decision often is the one that says 'no,' right? I've gotten a little way along on a project and I've realized that it's either (a) a lot more costly to build than I really thought, so I need to stop now before I'm knee deep in this, or (b) people are just not accepting it in the marketplace as we assumed, so again stop it earlier rather than later. If you build the whole thing and then decide they don't like it, you're in trouble.

There's nothing like learning from experience, which is how Lawrence Baxter has come to the following principle—

> A question that we ask outside consulting firms when they bid on projects for us is, 'Have you done this before?' We tell them, 'Please show us that you've done this before or we don't want to do it with you.' We've learned that there's so much discovery involved with a company that's learning on our time, that they don't bring us the help we need.
>
> That's particularly the case with any initiative that involves innovation. [In-house customers] naturally tend to be skeptical

of any new project that requires breaking new ground. We hear, 'Well, we haven't seen this done before.' We all know what happens when you embark on something that you're confident is going to save money but that you've not done before. It brings benefits in the long run but it may be a long road getting there.

If you're serious about holding your own feet to the fire on the governance issue, you can't escape taking on the responsibility of judging yourself—looking back and asking whether what you've done made good sense. "Sometimes," Lawrence said, "there are projects which I would hate to have the judgment of history on. There are some projects I'd like to claim I inherited, when the truth is at some point I've got to say, 'Well, I dragged my feet about this long enough, I can't blame anybody else anymore, I should have stopped it. This one is my responsibility.'"

In Baxter's view, accountability can become a problem because of a company's leadership development program, which flies in the face of what he calls "the golden handcuffs of tying people to positions so they don't move. We talk out of both sides of our mouths," he says, "because we also claim we're making sure everybody has an opportunity to advance. The skeptic will say that we waited until the person knew what they were doing in their job and then moved them out of that job, and called it professional advancement." In the process, project accountability gets lost.

New to the Governance Game

Among companies that have come to the game only recently, consider Airborne. Rachelle Mileur explained how things have changed—

> The $64,000 question looming now is we have so many people, our IT spends are growing very big, and enterprise wide. Should we go to [a new operating system]? That spend for us means not just software, but also computer upgrades for 35,000 colleagues. That's a lot of money.
>
> We go to senior leadership and say, 'We need to spend $12 million for this so everybody can be working with the current version.' Suppose that $12 million is a few percent of our budget. Management will ask, 'What will the new version do that the current one won't?' And that's where the governance process

really works. If we can say the current version will allow colleagues around the globe to collaborate, and will do these three other valuable things, then it's a pretty quick decision.

Before, IT would say, 'We need $12 million 'cause the new version has been released,' and the request would be approved. About two or three years ago they stopped giving an approval so easily. Senior leadership started to say, 'We need to hold expenses. If we don't really need the new version right now, put it off until next year.' Sometimes we can justify an expense by showing how this project will reduce full-time equivalents, or will reduce cycle time, so it's worth the $1.8 million.

But as Rachelle also pointed out, the bigger issue is whether the Airborne people would use this new tool. The questions facing every company in this situation include, "What questions do we need to ask to make sure our people want it, need it, will use it?" And, "How will we measure that they really do?"

An effective governance process offers the best answers.

Lessons from Companies with Successful Programs

As is true for a number of people whose insights appear in this book, I've known Washington Mutual's Jerry Gross for some time, and have observed the bank's introduction to the world of technology governance. The firm has become something of a model in the use of technology, so Jerry's input on the subject has special significance—

> Our Capital Expenditures Committee, which manages all of our expenditures, both technology and non-technology, is made up of myself, the CFO, and two other business segment presidents.
>
> We meet once a month and review projects over a certain dollar amount. The committee is essentially looking at all the capital expenditures enterprise-wide that cross business segments. And determining whether the investment makes sense based upon where the business is at that particular point in time. So the CapEx Committee is a key governance piece.
>
> Anyone who wants a technology project has to come in with a business plan already developed in order to get approval.

The other piece of this is that the CapEx Committee acts not only when the project is initiated but also in an on-going role as a reviewing body, because some of these projects may take nine months or twelve months to complete. We look at the on-going performance of these projects as part of the quarterly performance reviews when we sit down with each of the primary business units, and each reports their status and their performance for that quarter.

Technology is part of that, with its own quarterly business review, but that is something that happens after the businesses have done their reports to CapEx, and it's usually just addressing enterprise-wide issues as opposed to the specific business segment projects themselves.

The value of instituting a formal governance approach is no different whether your organization is a law firm, a coffin manufacturer, a railroad, or a county water district. Or a technology company. You might expect that a technology company would be smarter about governance than a company in some other field. In fact, that's often not the case.

Cisco, on the other hand, is a shining example of a technology company that has its act together. This is Cisco Senior Vice President Gary Moore:

> There is an Internet Capabilities Team at Cisco that is led by our CIO Brad Boston and Senior VP, Randy Pond, and it reports to [our CEO] John Chambers. Quarterly, every major business leader goes in and talks about what information technology they're implementing to improve productivity and run the business on the Internet. And jointly, the corporate systems are looked at by the CIO and his team, and they make decisions relative to platform and technology. So all major projects have to be approved at the highest level of the company.
>
> These projects are not funded by corporate, they're funded by the businesses, with perhaps some additional money from a corporate pool. Basically, though, our customer care systems are funded by our Customer Care organization, our financial systems are funded by the Finance Department, and so on. We call this a 'client-funded' model.
>
> And any new technology initiative gets driven by the business rather than by IT. It's a partnership, but it's driven by the business.

As the head of a business, from the technology point of view I have the ability to do almost anything I want to do, so long as I'm willing to fund it and it meets the corporate IT standards. The corporate IT group doesn't work on anything for my business that I don't specifically fund.

Also, they won't work on something unless I as the business leader have named a process owner, which is a somewhat unique approach.

So it's not about implementing an IT system, it's about how we're changing the process. And that's what's really important here. We're continually innovating not just technology, but the way we do things to drive a higher and higher level of productivity.

As I've moved around the world and talked to other executives, I find that an understanding of the need for governance is lacking in many places, but in many places a lot of people really get it. Jack Welch got it, Bill Gates and Steve Ballmer get it.

But you don't have to be Gates or a Ballmer to understand the need.

For the Chevron merger with Texaco mentioned earlier in these pages, Dave Clementz had an IT oversight group up to speed well before a final agreement had been reached between the two companies. From the first, the meetings of this group were frequent. And frequently virtual—

As the Chief Information Officer for the corporation, I have a CIO council that I preside over. The members are the CIO's for each of the four major operating arms. We would meet virtually, getting together on a conference call or a studio conference once a week to address the enterprise issues, things concerning issues like security, the digital desktop, the digital backbone, the telecom service. Anything that touched a large part of the enterprise, we took governance on.

My focus really is in technology management—executive coaching on the use of technology to enable the businesses to meet goals. That's the way we structured our business plan for our IT company.

Once the merger was finalized, a single corporate governance council was given responsibility for all internal technology projects. Unlike other councils that are limited to the approval and monitoring of projects, ChevronTexaco's has a broader scope—

The council presents a business plan each year, with goals, values, drivers, and metrics along the way. A lot of it has to do with people skills, technology for the future, and thinking about what we're going to do as an enterprise for the following year. We also get into things in the enterprise drive from the technology angles that are aimed at specific kinds of business problems. Right now, for example, security is a major issue, and [we need to ask] what we can do from an enterprise standpoint to cut the costs of providing security so everybody doesn't have to go out and find their own solutions.

So the IT company has a business plan and the CIO council creates an enterprise business plan. Each of those are aligned with the corporate business plan. We get guidance from the Corporate Planning Committee for our direction, and then sit down with them and review our performance at the end of the year. So last year in December I trotted over to meet with the Chairman and the Vice Chairman and the other folks on the Planning Committee, and I presented the results of our performance last year to them.

What the Executive Committee wants is the highlighted view. How far did we get with coverage? How fast did we get over some of the stumbling blocks to getting it deployed as fully as it could? What were the savings? And what were the significant warnings?

All of these are things you want to preserve as part of the record so you can carry the knowledge forward for the next big project.

One small tip that Dave Clementz offered is too good not to share—

Some of the things we learned from the first project done under the council that were really important were simple things, like helping people learn while you do a global installation. What we did is we made sure that while one country was doing their installation, some of our people from other countries in the region were on hand so they could learn what was going on. We always tried to have people from the next deployment taking part so they could understand how the architecture was laid out, how the machines went, how you unload and load, how you install software, and so on.

This really helps speed the process because they get to learn while doing, and when they get back to their country they've already been through one of these system installations, so it's not a big deal to do it again. So you get to propagate this knowledge across the world as you're going around.

At insurance brokerage firm Marsh, the demand for IT governance originated from senior leadership. "I put a good year and a half of my life into developing our first technology governance committee that worked," Roger Smith said. And he added, "It wasn't all rosy."

Among other things, Roger took a lot of heat from the business leaders. "People on the business side said in effect, 'Look, I'm a business leader, I know what I'm doing, how dare you question whether we'll use this or not, how dare you question if I have a process?' It was rough."

Roger was helped by having corporate leadership behind the idea of the IT governance council from the start—

The leadership in the company said, 'We need this.' One said, 'I have no way of knowing how valuable a technology investment is, other than what the business leader says to me. We have no basis to evaluate it from a technology standpoint. We don't have enough information to know whether it will really make a difference.'

I am hearing from two hundred leaders who all say their project should be approved. I am going to approve fifty projects a year and I simply cannot differentiate.

We've been working for the past three years to build this as a business-led governance process such that it's a partnership with technology; it's not 'us versus them.' Before that, IT frankly was in the dark as well. They said, 'We need business to tell us what the priorities are. Otherwise we have to listen to the most senior voice in the room; we have no choice.' It was—and I know many businesses run this way— whoever had the loudest voice at the table got their IT project through. We had little process for deciding on this one instead of that one.

Really quickly, we set up different thresholds of spending; up to a certain amount, the business can approve their own spend. Other thresholds go into the committee for approval.

And at a certain level or something that's going to be enter-prise-wide, the committee will want to meet with the business.

But we've gotten to the point now where it's not an onerous process. The governance group has eight business leaders from all over the U.S. The most senior of them now runs the North American operations for the firm. And they meet quar-terly. They're highly focused, they know where the firm needs to go, and they can put these applications through pretty good filters and give a quick response.

So much of the work is done before the committee sees the project that it's pretty easy to say 'yes' or 'no.' I could often vote to approve a project in five minutes because I had all the information.

It sounds as if creating the governance function at Marsh was focused entirely on whipping the business side into line. Not at all. IT came under the gun, as well—

Part of the pain with getting the governance process up and running was actually getting IT to be realistic about their spends. Just to use some figures for example, suppose IT had a $100 million technology budget. Some business unit would want to do a project and IT would say, 'We're out of money for the year.'

'What do you mean—you had $100 million.'

'Well, 98 million of it's for infrastructure.'

Business leaders also complained about some of IT's projects. They'd say, 'You're going to spend $2 million so eight hundred IT people can instant message themselves, and we're not going to enable clients to instant message into their client exec?'

That's why the even our senior IT leadership, prior to our new CIO coming on board last year, said that we needed a way to prioritize for the IT spend—some for infrastructure, some for cutting edge.'

As a member of the IT governance committee, a lot of the information that I needed to make my decision was based on [questions like], 'What's your process like now? What will it be like? How will it be embraced? How will the people be trained? And how will it be monitored? What will your picture of success be?'

And when I heard things like, 'Within six weeks of this being delivered, every person in the operation will be certified, anyone not certified will be locked out. And we will have different levels of certification, so that colleagues in Dallas with an agreed-upon level of training can actually handle a transaction for someone in London. The colleague in London will feel comfortable that the Dallas people are qualified, so the hand-off will take place.' At that point we'd recognized that they had really done thorough planning and we'd say, 'Okay, stop. You've convinced us, go do it.' When all of that work is done beforehand, the committee can simply say 'yes' or 'no'. This dialogue, and the decision to approve, took about 5 minutes. And yes, the application is very successful today.

Obviously there's dialog before the meeting. A business leader can talk to me as a committee member and say, 'Here's what I'm thinking of doing. Can you suggest anything else you would need to make a decision?' And I might say, 'That sounds like it could have global impact, have you spoken to so and so in France?' So there's advance guidance available all along the way.

One of the elements that Roger now says became a major factor in overcoming resistance to the concept of governance was to clarify what information a business leader would need to submit in order to gain approval for an IT project. Roger worked with corporate leadership to develop a series of questions that the head of a business unit would need to present in a business case before the governance council would consider any major IT project—

Business unit leaders had previously gone in and said, 'Spend millions, make billions.' In other words, if you do this technology project for me, the company will reap a huge payoff. They would say what they knew we wanted to hear. But we had no real way of prioritizing. And we always had many more requests than we had budget dollars for.

The business case methodology really helped because so much of it was not about technology—it was focused on getting answers to people and process questions. We knew we couldn't ask them questions that required them to be familiar with the technology, like, 'How long will it take to get this installed?'

But we could ask, and expect answers, to questions like: 'How many folks will use this? What's their level of competency? What's their functionality? How will this change your process? What are competitors doing? What are clients expecting?'

The smart business leaders took to it right away. With some others, we fought our battles the first few months and then everybody pretty much fell into line.

The preface to the template gives a set of goals in setting up a governance process for technology; reworded for our purposes, the goals include—

- Providing a process by which technology resources are allocated according to business priorities

- Providing technology projects with identifiable business ownership, with appropriate accountability, and with credible metrics for measuring ROI and monitoring results

- Insuring that the people, process and technology implications of proposed projects are fully understood and considered in the approval process

- Insuring that Marsh technology standards are leveraged to the fullest extent possible

- Insuring that Marsh's technology plans are widely understood and agreed upon by all Marsh technology stakeholders

It's worth noting that the Marsh business case template has about two pages on technology and about eight pages on people and process. (Roger has provided some excerpts, along with some useful pointers on how various items are used by the governance council; see the Appendix.)

These days, Marsh uses "working groups" for evaluating enterprise-wide technology projects—

The working groups are made up of business leaders. We try to be realistic about telling them in advance how much time will be involved; 'This will require three meetings, three hours each.' It's important that we have the time commitment.

This becomes a push-pull exercise. You know, the business will say 'We need a better process enabled by technology to accomplish certain tasks.' And we use this working group to make sure that they've thought it through. GE uses this phrase 'wing-to-wing,' which means not just delivering the engines, but looking at the entire process from start to finish.

The other thing is we also select a business project owner. I think that's the most important thing. I understand that

Microsoft does something similar, that you have a business owner who stays involved with the developers and meets frequently with them. That will catch the other maybe 10 to 20 percent of the requirements that weren't fully elaborated in the focus groups. So the developer might say, 'We've come up with this enhancement that when you hit this keystroke you get these three fields automatically populated.' And the business leader might respond, 'Oh, we should have told you we need a fourth field, and here it is.'

So we take the working group and say, 'Go back to the very beginning, when you start the relationship with a client, and then go to the very end, maybe five or six steps after you've completed the process, and tell us what happens.' Just to make sure that we haven't missed anything that should be in the technology, and also to make certain we are enabling the right process. This prevents a lot of scope creep. It helps prevent missing something, delivering the wrong product, delivering something that won't really accomplish what the business didn't realize they needed.

Also, we actually look for perceived obstacles—responses like, 'If it doesn't do X, I can't use it.' You take those objections and you see how realistic they really are. A lot of it is about change and change management—we're trying to avoid building a technology that perpetuates a less effective way of doing things. We try to address valid issues in the design phase so that when the technology is rolled out, these are no longer issues.

We'll also do some vetting if it seems to be needed when we get objections, or 'It must do this.' 'Why does it have to do that?' 'Oh, because Sam wants a report.' 'Oh why does Sam want a report?' 'I don't know, he just always asks me for a report.' 'What does he do with it?' 'I don't know.' So sometimes we get into the work processes and find out what's really going on.

However, working groups can confuse the issue—

There's an area where a working group can lead us astray, because we tend to look at segments. If our large customers who buy more consultative services say this would be nice to have, but our more transactional customers—where the volume would be—wouldn't use it, we need to take a hard look at the value proposition. We have to make a judgment call.

Consequently, we need to populate the working group with a broad enough representation so that decisions are not over-weighted.

One thing that's unique about Marsh as opposed to most other large companies is that while many of their offices function as branches, they're actually more like separate businesses within their own geographic area—

> Just the way Los Angeles and San Francisco are different communities within California, our offices are somewhat a mirror image of the way business is done in those two cities. So we developed the practice of taking polls through the company, getting a geographic spread.
>
> But that could have us just sitting there and saying, 'We can't do this anywhere because our offices are all so different.' So we tried to achieve an intersection of different needs by telling everyone, in effect, 'Here's an initiative that we must do consistently across the U.S. What, if any, are the geographic differences or nuances of the program that need to be tailored for your city or your region?'
>
> The bottom line is, when it's rolled out, the technology does pretty much what everyone who had a strong opinion wanted it to do. The goal is for people to say, 'Wow!' and 'Thanks.'

Take-Aways

So, what are the elements that should be part of any governance process?

A number of things must occur for governance to work. To begin with, you have to have an agreed-upon process up front on how you will assess what the business argument is. Whether you call it cost/benefit, or return on investment, or effectiveness, or efficiency—whatever, you have to decide in advance what yardstick you will use. Governance also calls for an agreement on how you're going to manage something, to guide yourself through some process. And if the focus is business value, you better start by defining at the outset what the devil you mean by "business value," and how you're going to assess the potential for it.

Effective governance also requires setting priorities. The constant debate over which projects should and shouldn't get done, the decisions based on who yells loudest, and so on, ought to be something of the past. You need to be deciding among projects on the basis of which ones have the closest link to the business priorities.

And then comes the question of who will own the business case. I know I'm repeating myself here, but some one person has to be designated, who will stand before the board and say, "This is what we want to do, this is what it will cost, this is what the benefits will be, and I'm the person taking the responsibility." Not to hammer the point to death, but, again, this must be somebody from the business side, not from the technology group. This should be Rule Number One: the business case is owned by the business side of the house.

I would add to the items offered by the people quoted above about what issues should be addressed up front in the governance process. The element I want to see included is this: as part of the issue of accountability, what will happen if the project turns out to be a disaster, or even if it only turns out to be a failure on some smaller scale? Will the project owner have his pay docked? Or receive a black mark on his next review? Or what? The reward for success and the penalty for failure should, in my view, be clear to everybody from the get-go.

Beside the project owner who has overall responsibility, you will also need to make a decision about selecting the person will be responsible for day-to-day managing of the project. The project manager says who's responsible for the process change that may have to occur, who's responsible for the personnel decisions, and who's responsible for the technical implementation—which is almost always the least challenging part of any project, but where people often spend most of their time. You need to see the manager's job as an issue of managing an entire project, not just implementing some new technology.

Any effort of the scale we're talking about here needs to have checkpoints established. No checkpoints means no accountability until the project is finished, or is in such bad trouble that everyone starts running around in circles. Checkpoints should be a no-brainer.

Finally, the audit—that process we've talked about in earlier chapters for agreeing in advance how you will measure to what degree the project was successful in achieving the promised benefits. The audit becomes the key ingredient for closing the governance loop.

I hope it's clear that a governance process endorsed and accepted by senior management is a requirement if the resulting business cases and audits are going to have any validity. This is an effort that requires visible support from the top, and it needs to apply to all on an equal basis across the organization.

An active, effective governance process is no longer a choice but a necessity.

7

"The Beatings Will Continue Until the Culture Improves"

> There was an attitude of some of the people who were near retirement that 'I don't have to learn this stuff and you can't make me. I've been doing it this way for 35 years, I'll do it this way for two more.'
>
> —Lt. General Steven Boutelle, *Army CIO*

If, as I believe, some of the biggest benefits from technology come about only if an organization is willing to change how it has worked historically, culture becomes a central issue. Companies that manage to be nimble about changing with the market conditions turn out to be the most successful.

Thinking about whether your business has to change to meet the changing environment is critical for success; that much is obvious. Less obvious is the idea that an organization's willingness to change is critical to whether they will reap benefits from investments in technology. Or, for that matter, investments in anything. But because major technology investments are so large; and because technology is not of value itself, but only to the degree that it enables people to work differently and more effectively, it becomes of paramount importance that the people of the organization do not feel threatened by change. And that's a cultural issue.

Truly understanding your company's culture and working within it is critical to gaining benefits. In doing the interviews for this book, the question of culture was a frequent subtext underlying other issues. For example, Wachovia's Lawrence Baxter—

I've become more and more aware that business requirements are now a frequently recurring source of friction between IT and business units. That friction is often the reason given for the delay in going into production with new services that are technology based.

My first naive approach was, people need thorough requirements training, and they need to use the requirements tool we've created. Let's get them on board.

But the more I looked at it, the more I saw that we have achieved a good level of awareness on the business side for the importance of technology 'with a big T.' On the other hand, I don't think we've achieved a level of thinking about the business practice of technology yet. By which I mean that, when strategy is being formulated in a traditional company like ours, I don't think that business folks think through what that means in terms of how they have to act differently to achieve the benefits that they're expecting from some new piece of technology.

So 'a big T' means everybody in Wachovia knows technology is important and everybody now wants the IT department to account for their investments. We now track whether the value promised by IT was ever fully captured with projects.

Lawrence says that everybody on the business side is becoming acutely aware of finding out whether the promised business value was achieved "because they've learned how expensive IT is." Even so, they've only taken the first step—

Have they changed the way in which business is done, the way in which these sales forces are trained, and they way in which the product managers think about and report up their deployment of product? I don't think that's happened much at all.

But nobody is pointing a finger at Wachovia as an example of failure in this area. Lawrence is aware of the problem; he and many others in Wachovia are making inroads, while a lot of other companies have a great deal less success to show. Maybe it's not surprising, but the same culture gap—in spades—happens in the military. Carla von Bernewitz:

When I came to work for a military department, the first thing I learned was that there's a huge difference between the warfighter side of the house, which we call operational, and the other side, which is the support or the business-function side—

though Army people don't like to use the word 'business,' because the Army is not a business.

Technology as a Catalyst for Changing the Business

Often the most significant benefit associated with technology comes from its role as a catalyst. That happens when we intentionally use technology to change how we do business—for example, by threatening current core processes, blowing up and getting rid of some of them, changing them dramatically, changing a whole organization. Wachovia's Lawrence Baxter holds the view that using technology to bring about change just hasn't happened as it should have—

> I don't think technology has significantly changed the way we've done business except in certain areas, like those well publicized areas where supply chains have been revolutionized. But for the most part, when we do a technology deployment there's still very little innovative process change that's brought to bear on it. It's more replication of the old environment at a faster pace, but a more expensive one.
>
> I think we're not very good as humans at translating this into really effective productivity because we've neglected how we change our own personal and cultural behavior to accommodate technology.
>
> We've almost hijacked the technology to speed up our behaviors, as opposed to thoughtfully reinventing our behaviors. And I think that when you get to the place where you're leveraging the technology for your businesses, often there's not a whole lot there that's actually new, it's just faster.

Lawrence went on to make a comment that he prefaced by saying I would probably laugh at "because you're surrounded by it all the time." Based on his visits to Microsoft for the executive conferences that he has attended. He said—

> One tends to have grand thoughts when you get out to Redmond. It gives you a chance to think and start imagining some grand things. It's like the Aspen Institute, a great center for learning—in this case learning about the change of business behavior that's brought about by technology.

There's a whole new role that's probably opening up, and not just for leadership. It seems to be a form of behavior-changing education. I want to carefully avoid the clichés because it would then just be written off by all those of us in business who are really looking for excuses not to have to do different each day what we do because we're already beleaguered and rushed and pressured. But we almost need to come up with something like Covey's 'Seven Habits' for the business practice of technology. Maybe we need to get people coming straight out of B-school, actually teach them a whole structure of strategic analysis, different from the way it is now—so that when they think, for example, about increasing sales in a certain area, they'll think about how technology could be used to do it.

The Army CIO, Lt. General Boutelle, agrees on the problem of convincing people to be open to technology change—

I can remember in my old organization there was an attitude of some of the people who were near retirement that 'I don't have to learn this stuff and you can't make me. I've been doing it this way for 35 years, I'll do it this way for two more.' When I started as a project manager of digital systems in 1992, it was the second lieutenants and first lieutenants who got it, and it was the colonels, lieutenant colonels, and majors who were generally clueless. Now we're up to the point where it's the majors and lieutenant colonels who get it.

The Army, contrary to some beliefs, is a very corporate-like structure, with very difficult challenges when you try to change the culture. If you look at the age of our workforce, which is similar to a lot of industry, we have something close to 80 percent of our senior leaders, both civilian and military, who will retire in the next four to six years.

Some people say this is terrible and the sky is falling. But out of several hundred intern positions opening up, we have several thousand college graduates applying for them. We have superstars coming in at the bottom. They don't have 35 years of experience, but that's not all bad. Because what we find is that many of us who are more senior hold to a culture that is not readily adaptable to the information technology era.

As the General sees it, this move of the Baby Boomer generation out of government is helping the Army tremendously in the change of culture—helping them adapt to today's pervasive information society—

> The culture now has just come to the realization—especially as a result of the Afghanistan and Iraq operations—that IT and networking really have not only tremendous value, they're the Holy Grail. People are not saying 'IT,' they're saying 'network centric.' The culture is now finally catching up with what that technology has been able to do in tying all these systems together—ships, airplanes, ground units, and command centers, all the way back to the homeland in the United States.
>
> But also, the good news is that within every generation you do have some of the senior leaders that get it, who understand the new and the need to change. Now, do they understand the technology? No. Do they understand the power of the technology? They grasp that very quickly. We've been very fortunate that we've always had a few of those at the very top, the four stars [four-star general and admirals, the highest current rank of the U.S. military] who understand that power of technology.
>
> In the book *Unleashing the Killer App,* which Larry Downes, Chunka Mui, and Nicholas Negroponte did a couple of years ago, they claim that the culture lags about two years behind the technology. That's probably a pretty good metric.

At Microsoft, Bill Gates is adamant about insuring that many new people join the company each year fresh from the college campus, to keep us constantly pressured with that kind of fresh blood and fresh thinking—very similar to what Lt. General Boutelle was talking about.

At the same time, the general's deputy, Dave Borland, reminds us that the Army needs urgently—even more urgently than your company or mine—to be to be using technology more effectively, while still keeping technology costs very much in check—

> The Army has recognized the fact that if we're going to do as much as we've been asked to do by the country over the past ten years—and by the way, it's remarkable when you count up the number of deployments the Army has had in the past ten or fifteen years—then we're going to have to spend less money on information and more money on preparing ourselves for these missions. We've had a Chief of Staff of the Army and a

Secretary of the Army who have both mandated the notion of centralized personnel systems, centralized logistics systems, centralized financial system, centralized installation management system—all delivered over a centrally managed information technology infrastructure. That's from the top. Everybody in the Army now understands that.

Carla von Bernewitz described the issue this way—

Our philosophy is to make change by buying this or that software, and the software has in it these embedded best business practices, so we will adopt those business processes. When the software is installed, we simply do business that way. Of course, the software allows you to select various models of business practices.

But if you don't have some adult supervision of what's going on in those projects, you're really going to end up with your father's Oldsmobile, and there's a real danger in that.

Professor Schlenker of the Ecole de Management commented that "When we focus million dollar investments on technology, it's easy to forget that they need to be a reflection of the way we work." And he went on to highlight yet another aspect of making technology serve its users:

The shortcomings of these systems aren't necessarily technical, but in forgetting the essential fact that they're there to help people work better. They mirror what people do well and what people don't do well. And when you forget that lesson, you start looking at technology for the sake of technology, and you run into million-dollar wastes.

There's also a belief in the practice of "one best way"—that if it worked in 300-odd best-practice firms, it will work in your firm. You end up with companies ignoring their own managers' claims of the uniqueness of their own company culture to suit the needs of the software.

I think one of the important points is that your managers and employees don't necessarily want to be like everyone else, they want to be better than anyone else. And that's one of the things that ERP software doesn't do for you. If it fits your company's needs perfectly, which is rarely case, it helps you to, at best, be as good as everyone else.

Comparative advantage comes from putting into place processes that meet client needs in a way that's either better than those of the competition, or somehow unique. But when you're using exactly the same processes as everyone else, you don't automatically have a basis for competitive advantage. That's why collaborative technologies are going to be so important—they feed a corporate culture dependent on client relationships that are unique, coming from the strengths of the talent or the knowledge that you have within the firm. This provides your company with a basis for competitive advantage.

Making Change Happen

Change is hard, and always will be. Facing that truism, some organizations have found wisdom in creating a group dedicated on a full-time basis to insuring that technology-induced culture changes take place smoothly. As ChevronTexaco's Dave Clementz put it, "We actually now have a change management group in our company on the delivery side, and that's all they do. They work on change management processes. And as you get a network connected the way we have now, it becomes even more critical to have rigorous processes, because a small change here is going to have a big effect somewhere you haven't even figured out."

In many cases, Rick Greenwood reminds, the CIO himself needs to be directly involved in managing change. "A lot of times technology people can't help having the attitude, 'This is really cool and glitzy,' and that can lead to doing a terrible job of tying the technology to a business value proposition. But one of the big parts of the CIO's role is the relationship aspect—helping people keep the issues straight."

This is a man who is apparently getting respect from his senior executives as a result of thinking creatively about how the business could change. He's an enabler of technology, but the responsibility has expanded beyond that: he also serves in a consultant or advisory role, thinking about things such as what new revenue streams might be possible.

The approach at Washington Mutual, according to CIO Jerry Gross, "is all about process."

Inside the IT organization, we have an operational excellence function you don't often see. Let's say, for example, we're rolling out a new capability on our website. Our Product Management Group takes responsibility for collaboration—full end-to-end responsibility of the implementation and deployment, which includes training, change management, documentation, feedback loops, etc.

The process piece is key; it's all about process. You can throw hardware at something or software at something, but you have to have change management processes and key learning processes, and feedback loops surrounding any of the technology that you put in place—recovery restart, disaster recovery, security processes. All of these items have to go along with any technology that we're implementing.

The easiest piece of all is the technology itself. I say the least important element is the actual technology.

ChevronTexaco's Dave Clementz says that he has always been fascinated by technology, but only by the part he calls the "so what" elements: "If we do this, so what will it mean for our people and for the company? If we provided hand-helds for everyone in the field, so what would the benefits be?" He looks at an expense and wants to know, "How is this going to pay off?" Once he has figured out why the company needs some particular piece or effort, he wants to know, "What would drive us to change without it?" Those, he says, are the questions he always asks. And of course there's no Okay until he's satisfied with the answers.

The CIO of the Army has a different approach to the process for bringing new technology into the existing culture—

One piece that we have done very successfully in the past is having a structured process [for evaluating new technology]. Very structured in the fact that we had planned experiments, and the theme of these was always to invite all the people and organizations out there to bring in new technologies. Put them in an operational environment. Take them through an experiment. And then cull out the ones that we want to further deal with.

We could buy the technology immediately and put it into the Army. We could take the idea to our technology base for a little bit more work on it and create a plan on when we can bring it into use. Or we could say, 'this doesn't fit and we don't have any need for it.'

Today we're more heavily involved in joint experimentation. JiffCom, the Joint Forces Command, has been empowered by the Secretary of Defense and the Congress to become heavily committed to on-going experimentation. So it's JiffCom that deals with how you shape those experiments to bring in commercial technologies. Then the challenge is how to quickly turn them into use in the services; that's the hard part.

The vision statement of Army technology, from General Boutelle's office, makes change an essential ingredient of the organization's focus, with a phrase that calls for "being the strategic change agent for world-class, network-centric, knowledge-based capabilities." The Army's Dave Borland expanded on the significance of the statement—

That really puts forward two messages. One of them is an acknowledgement that the Army's CIO supports the large, substantive transformation that the Army is undergoing, while at the same time honoring our contract to do whatever it takes to handle current crises.

The Army we had five or six years ago was designed to meet and defeat the Russians at the Fulda Gap. And what we have now is a whole lot of things like Iraq, like Bosnia, like some of the things that are going on in South America. Lots of hot spots around the globe. So it's vastly different than what we had built our Army for.

The objective today is to make our Army more agile, more quick thinking, and more lethal at the same time. In order to do that, in order to be able to be flexible, in order to be able to change a plan, you've got to be able to command-and-control quickly. You've got to be able to provide situational awareness down as far as you can in the organization.

We're aggressively pursuing change in not only our organization structures but in our doctrine, in the ways we plan to fight the kinds of fights we think will happen in the future, which are definitely different than what we've done in the past.

That's IT as an enabler of changing tactics, changing doctrine, and changing organization. "Two weeks after I arrived here [at Army headquarters]," Carla von Bernewitz said, "the realization was that the way we had done things in the past—whether you were talking systems or organizational change or how we were going to do business—had not provided enough linkage between the business side and the war-fighter side, very little doctrine about how they're going to do things."

She observed that there had been a lot of progress made in terms of bringing the Army together as one enterprise for the war-fighter side, but noted that "there was not the same thing happening on the back-office side because that's not what we go to Congress and say we need more money for. We don't get kudos for building another financial system. We get kudos for winning the next war."

Wachovia's Lawrence Baxter offered an amusing observation that highlights one aspect of the need for change, growing out of a problem raised repeatedly in these pages: the gulf that still exists between the business side and the technology folks. He says, "The whole structure of the way people think about strategic analysis needs to be different from the way it is now. Today I see examples all the time of business people who will think about, say, a solution for increasing the sales in a certain area, and they'll do a strategy paper that has a little bullet near the end saying 'Leverage online platform.' It's almost funny when you see it. Everybody knows they must leverage the online platform, but few on that team could give you any idea of what they mean by the statement."

As if they think that somebody in IT will just push a button and the technology will happen. Lawrence offers a suggestion: "To some extent it requires a rethinking of what leverage really means in business sales terms. It's a different way of thinking about how to go to market. It's not just more and faster of the same."

Once again from Carla von Bernewitz, this time a description of how her office lays the groundwork in advance of change—

> For me personally, it's called communication. A lot of times people make decisions when they don't have all the information and don't know what else is going on around them. And especially in a large organization, you've got your head down and you're full steam ahead working on what you're responsible for—that's how you get the job accomplished. And if you get sidetracked by what somebody else is doing, then you won't accomplish what you need to do.
>
> Yet I'm really in there basically sidetracking folks, because I'm asking questions like, 'Well, have you talked to so and so who's doing something similar?' Or, 'If this particular business change comes down, how are you going to address it?' So a lot

of what we are doing here is communicating on getting people ready to cope with issues that are just about to surface.

One other culture issue that comes up repeatedly: dealing with technology budget cuts. Dave Clementz—

> The company says, 'Cut 30 percent,' so it gets applied evenly across the organization. But if you do that with your IT organization, you might as well close your doors—it will drive so many critical functions subcritical that you won't be able to do anything innovative.
>
> So what we had to do was run a study to figure out segments of technology that could be completely outsourced, eliminated, or provided for by alliances with external providers, and which ones do we really need to keep inside. We went through that exercise, and found places where we could make changes. In the end we gave the company back not 30 percent, but 40 percent.

Steve Hankins reported that at Tyson Foods, he finds executives playing the head-count card—

> I'm in the meat industry, which is not a high margin industry. Management in our industry has a tendency to equate all costs with head count. Even the more enlightened ones will fall back to judging in terms of head count. When there's a reduction, they can see that—it's a hard cost, people disappeared.
>
> You can do calculations around that and other costs such as improving cycle time. But many times management will see a technology benefit as a saving in a soft cost. And a lot of times they'll throw that out and get upset because they don't see an opportunity to cut workers.

No matter how you slice it, people who bring new technology into their company need to develop skills in the art of dealing with change and in the techniques of making change acceptable.

Culture Change in a Company with Many Divisions or Subsidiaries

While everyone agrees that an organization benefits from a culture that is uniform throughout its units, departments, and groups, it's less obvious how that same reasoning applies as well to the technology culture. The problem tends to be greater if growth has come about through mergers or acquisitions. After going through the process at CommonHealth, Craig Cuyar came to believe that achieving this consistency demands agreeing on a common way of how to manage change—

> We're in the middle of deploying SharePoint Portal across the enterprise, and have to deal both at the collective group level and with the individual CommonHealth companies, and there has to be a different 'sales' process for getting cooperation from each. Initially we shopped the idea around to two or three of the companies. One of them turned their nose up at it and said, 'No, not interested—it's beta code, we don't want to waste our time with that.' Another really didn't understand what the benefits would be, despite our efforts to explain. The third grabbed onto it right away, saying, 'This is exactly what we need.'
>
> So the sales process to get it into the individual unit is very different from how I sell it at the organization level. There I'm selling different value and different benefits as a collective organization. In the SharePoint model, I talk about how we can put portals in place that would be externally accessible to clients, and how we could deposit collateral digital assets into those systems, and provide external access to that portal environment for mobile staff members. But at the individual business unit level, I have to drill down into how this relates to that particular unit, the people within it, and the particular clients that it serves.
>
> Once we're able to sell it into one or two units and then build a case study that both quantifies and qualifies the value, then it's fairly easy to sell it to other units. And I can tell you, I already have two other business units that have come to me to say, 'Hey, where are we in the pecking order for that implementation?'

Many people come to the conclusion that the most important piece of toting up the value of a technology investment is the degree to which it brings about change. Jerry Gross embellished an earlier comment by remarking, "The three primary pieces to building a technology solution are people, process, and technology. The people piece is all about making sure you focus on the behaviors of the end users and understand what it's going to take to get them totally enabled in the technology."

While others tend to complain about the people piece, in Dave Borland's view, the Army sees the culture of their "workers in uniform" in a brilliant light—

One of the things we keep hearing about in the Army is our NCO Corps. People talk about the Noncommissioned Officer Corps in the United States Army as being the difference between this army and other armies of the world. The fact is that these NCOs are of such high quality that they're able to make logical decisions instead of following the last order from the last officer.

The IT role in this is that we are now providing a situational awareness down to that level where soldiers actually in the middle of executing orders can see what's going on 360 degrees around them, and what's going on 360 in the air above them. I think that's part of the reason that you saw what you saw on television in the initial part of the Iraq operation.

So if we in the Army IT community are going to support that bigger Army vision of a more agile, more lethal force, then we have to employ technology in a different way than we have before. We have to become more network centered to the point where everything we know is available to everybody. And we have to get it there at the speed of light.

In earlier times, a manager was somebody who had access to information that the workers on the factory floor, for example, were not privy to. It's been one of the landmark changes in the computer age that the more everyone in the organization is given access to information, the more productive and successful the company will be—

If you think about the way the Army operates and has been organized, managers in the Army don't do, they lead. The rest of us provide the people who 'do' with the support, tools, and so forth, to get their jobs done. So on both the combat side and the workaday side, that has been a change. Leading just isn't enough any more.

It's clear the military is using technology to enable its front-line forces. Is industry keeping up? Jerry Gross again raised the issue of people—this time not in terms of employees but as customers—

The customer experience is what it's all about. One report said that there's a direct correlation between customer satisfaction and employee enablement. When you enable the employee, that employee is more satisfied, which in turn translates into customer satisfaction. You can sense that when you talk to an employee of, say, Southwest Airlines; that's more of an enabled employee than perhaps if you talk to an employee of a more traditional airline, right?

Some of that has got to do with technology, but some of it also has to do with the culture of how the company uses its measurement systems and how it compensates employees. Everything we're doing is focused on enabling our employees. Everything else falls into place when a company has that nailed down.

Take-Aways

To be successful in getting people to accept the kinds of change we talk about in this chapter, every company needs to make a determined effort to communicate clearly about two aspects in particular: what the end-game is, and what role they play in it.

More than that, company communications need to be honest. The change we're talking about happening here is at the core of what many people worry most about. It implies a change in the familiar ways of doing things, often for long periods of time. And the possibility of reorganization. And even of job loss.

This is a leadership challenge that needs to rely on open communication and honesty with the people who are going to be impacted by technology changes so they can understand the role that they play and the potential that they have to grow as a result of the experience.

Still, you can't hide from the fact that there will be some disorientation. In fact, in some IT projects, productivity will go down in the early phases. People who have not been bought up to speed on the 'why' and the end-game, and how they are personally going to be impacted, will likely stand in the way. They will also be the ones saying "I told you so" as soon as the new whatever begins to hit the normal, expected kinds of snags. And the people who up front said, "It's not broken, why don't they just leave it alone" will chuckle at how wise they were.

Microsoft went through a change process led by CEO Steve Ballmer himself, which after a few years is still in process. It calls on the executive staff to rethink the core values of the company and then be hard on ourselves about what we need to do in order to get where we want to go in the future. This kind of rethinking about some of the key elements of the organization's culture can represent one of the biggest challenges for any company to face. Those companies that Jim Collins identified as "great" in his marvelous book *Good to Great* had each faced this hurdle. Making that leap from being a successful company to a great one, Collins showed, required among other steps the willingness to rethink the culture and recognize elements that require modification or even elimination. Understanding culture and how it can be used to encourage change will be a key determinate in whether an organization reaps the benefit it should from technology investments.

Leadership, communications, and honesty. People emulate their leadership.

Culture starts at the top.

8

Why Aren't You Using the "Ruby Slippers" Approach?

> [IT's] value proposition is not about the technology we bring; it's about the ability to understand all the business.
>
> —Rick Greenwood, *GMAC-RFC*

Former Microsoft VP Joe Eschbach uses a metaphor that he describes as "ruby slippers thinking." He points out that in *The Wizard of Oz*, Dorothy walked all over Oz; she fought flying monkeys, she threw water on a witch, and other crazy things, in her desperate effort to find a way of getting home. All the while she was wearing the ruby slippers—so she had the tool she needed literally at her feet to get her home whenever she wanted to. What she needed, Joe says, was best-practices knowledge—someone to tell her, "You've got the tool." In the same way, I may be agonizing over some business problem while the laptop in front of me has the data and the software to manipulate it, if I only knew it was there and what to do.

So "ruby slippers thinking" is the notion that we need to start making things discoverable. We need to let people know that they are already wearing the slippers—they have at hand the answers they're looking for.

Joe also points out that part of the problem is knowing you have a problem. Dorothy needed to know there was a place she could go, somebody she could talk to. The copying machine, voicemail—until somebody invented those things, nobody realized that doing without them was an inconvenience, a problem in our personal lives and a whopper of a problem in business.

Professor Lee Schlenker suggests that management theory and story telling are much alike. The primary value in a story, he maintains, is to get the reader to focus on something essential. That's the same goal as management theory. Solving problems of running IT—including problems that most people haven't even recognized yet—is the subject of this chapter.

The New Role of IT

Several of the folks we talked to sounded a note about the changing role of IT that reinforces a theme by now familiar in these pages. Rick Greenwood of GMAC-RFC's Residential Capital Group—

> IT has evolved from being order takers, to advisors, to being key influencers, to being key decision makers. And each is a step in the progression you have to go through. But it's never as a stand-alone; it always needs to be in partnership with the business.
>
> I think a lot of times what happened in the past was that IT was the sole decision maker without the business really understanding what we were trying to do.
>
> Our value proposition is not about the technology we bring; it's about the ability to understand all the business. Our ability to provide legitimacy to process control allows the other executives to have the agility that they desire to be competitive or to transform the environment.
>
> For us, that's understanding the businesses well enough that we can think, 'Here's the agility that they need, here are the things that we need to connect, and how we can control that in a way that's not going to prevent or impede, but will legitimatize what they're trying to do.' That's the gate you need to open.

Another view, this time from Wachovia Bank's Lawrence Baxter: "Traditional leadership has always been framed on the sports model of personal discipline: focus and dedication, setting an example, and so on. But IT doesn't seem yet to have developed enough pressure on executive teams. Some leaders have not ever thought about how to do technology differently, and they don't show the commitment needed to do it differently."

Craig Cuyar described how CommonHealth has tackled the problem by restructuring IT. "We've tried to flip our IT organization so we have groups that are focused on process and are working with the individual business units to improve process, reduce costs, implement systems that will provide overall efficiency, provide greater revenue potential, etc. And we've separated that from the utility function."

To Rachelle Mileur, one of the strengths of IT at Airborne reflected the company's structure as a very centralized organization, with the business side of the company closely aligned to the IT side, allowing for easy collaboration between the two in setting the direction of new technology. "I have easy access to our business decision makers," she says. "We work together very collaboratively for setting direction. This has been true for quite some time at Airborne. Technology is more often serving the business needs of the company instead of the other way around."

But many companies follow a painful course before they arrive at a formula for IT that makes sense within the corporate structure and culture. One has been Chevron, before Dave Clementz became CIO. He recalled—

> The IT organization in our firm grew up in the Finance department. So they were experts in counting the money, and they were very good at running large data centers, and so on. And then the operation was spun off as a separate company about sixteen years ago. And they were supporting Finance—it was one of their customers.
>
> IT was a big deal, it took a lot of resources, a lot of time and a lot of money. And I think during that period they just became so enamored with these big computer systems and keeping these big things alive, they lost focus. For example, the desktop environment—they were very slow to get into the common operating environment concept. They had it but they were still thinking big computers, client/server kind of environments for the longest time.
>
> They slowly got into this other thing, but what had happened is the operating companies got so disgruntled with the central organization's offerings, they were frustrated about the service quality and the expense, that they just built their own IT units.

In the period leading up to the Chevron merger with Texaco, Dave had been focused on reorganizing IT in an effort to drive down costs—

We had already done a lot prior to the merger in squeezing the Chevron IT budget. From the time I took over, I had taken the cost for the central IT group down from about $400 million a year to about $320 million.

That was based on four things—outsourcing a large chunk of the non-strategic work for lowered cost and higher leverage...driving common standards across the desktop, which really saved a big chunk of money...reorganizing around the portfolio, getting rid of things that weren't recovering costs...and then creating a new business model.

Another issue raised in one of our interviews on this subject will sound familiar because it's an underlying theme of this book. Integris Health CEO Stan Hupfeld said, "I think that a point we're trying to learn is making the operational people responsible for the success or failure of IT. A success or failure is not an IT success or failure: the operational people own it. It's a utility. I think for us this was somewhat of an 'ah-ha' that we're just coming to, and trying to focus on."

An admission from the CEO of a billion dollar organization that this is what he calls "an ah-ha" is an eye-opener. His commitment to change how they think about this issue in terms of responsibility—that is not the norm. Again, I think a failure to hold the business managers responsible for IT projects is one of the biggest impediments to reaping the kind of return people say they want from technology.

The Strategy of Running IT as a Business

Even within an organization dragging its feet about cultural change, IT can institute change on its own—blowing up some of its current core processes, getting rid of what's not working, changing others, change its organization. In the best of all worlds, corporate leadership learns to see IT as a strategic tool for doing business. Mary Kay's Kregg Jodie—

Even though there still may be some companies where technology is not as strategic as it is in other companies, because it's a fairly high-dollar amount, management of this expensive asset is a critical role for any executive team. It should not be left as a function lying under two or three levels of executives.

I don't think our approach to IT has changed the fundamental culture of Mary Kay, which is a very high-touch, people-oriented business. But I think that the characteristics of what we're expecting inside of IT have changed over the years, and throughout our organization you'll certainly find a high expectation of IT.

At Mary Kay, the rethinking went beyond just including the CIO in strategy sessions. "The members of the executive team were all doing the strategic business planning," Kregg explained. He continued—

Today, I help facilitate that, and help the [executive] team to think of ways that technology can enable portions of the strategic plan. Coming from a consulting background, I understood that you could not separate business process from technology. In fact, you must think of people management, processes, and technology together to achieve the desired result. Mary Kay is doing a good job at that, and it is truly a team effort.

I certainly think it's unusual for a CIO to be coordinating strategic planning, but it's a good fit because it helps the CIO stay in sync with the strategic direction of the company. The strategic direction is being driven from the top in terms of what we need to do, and clearly it's easy for me to determine the direction we should take with our technology.

When there are questions, the executive team makes those decisions—the CIO doesn't. But in most cases, we're focused on the same things.

Though the arrangement is somewhat unusual, I think you are getting more and more CIOs who are business driven, yet with enough technology background to couple these duties together.

Archie Kane highlighted a different issue—

The challenge is in building strategies, identifying your key strategic assets, and then identifying the core competencies that allow you to leverage your assets. An asset for us would be our very large customer base. Others would be our very wide distribution and our huge assembly of customer data. We can leverage those, or we can have somebody leverage them for us better than we can.

My point is that technology itself is not a core asset that we have which differentiates us from anybody else. It isn't a core competence that would allow us to compete better than anybody else.

We have one of the strongest distribution capabilities in this country, but if we don't get good IT support, we won't be able to leverage that distribution asset. So I see it as more as part of our overall set of competencies that will allow us to leverage our strategic assets.

The Army's Carla von Bernewitz offered a worthwhile reminder about this issue that applies to many companies—a hold-back-the-dawn attitude that afflicts many organizations (not including the U.S. Army), and that can stand in the way of change: "We've been winning wars; why would we want to change a winning thing?" Every organization, she reminds us, "has a culture and a way of doing business that's unique," and this is often a barrier to using technology intelligently.

She points to another often-overlooked issue as well—

We have so many things going on, but there's an actual outcome expected from these efforts. And just because somebody got out of the starting gates first doesn't mean that something else can't prevail at a later date. A lot of times you're going to sub-optimize a particular business unit, or function, or organization for the greater good of the entire enterprise. And that's a hard one to swallow; often it takes somebody from outside a particular business unit to see that that's what's needed.

Very often you'll find that a good idea gets started in a particular business unit or a particular functional area. And it's great for them, but then it stays within the walls of that unit and never goes any further. So you can have things that don't come from the top of the organization.

On the other hand, a new idea still has to be sponsored from the top of the business unit—finance or HR, for example. But if you're going to see the true impact across the entire enterprise, then the impetus has to come from the top.

It seems to be nearly universal that one yardstick for the success of a technology project measures how much the head count was reduced. Not everyone agrees that's a valid measure. Steve Hankins explained that in recent years Tyson Foods expanded business from $2 billion, to $4 billion, to $7 billion, with hardly any increase in the number of sales coordination people, tracking people, traffic management people, or the like:

We were able to do that because the technology stayed robust enough, and by adding EDI technology and different ways of executing the same processes that were driven by technology. So we didn't have to increase the number of people to get a lot more throughput.

The other executives went on faith around some of those technology efforts. When they looked through the rearview mirror and found case examples where they could see those types of [cost saving] returns, we got a lot of credibility from that to continue doing other things.

The one that was most interesting at Tyson was in the mid-nineties when we wanted to automate our first major warehouse. We planned to get a new warehouse management system and put in wireless. The guy on the forklift would look at his little handheld and it would tell him what to go do next. There would be a total elimination of the old paper-based process.

Although the benefits were clear, Steve still had some convincing to do. When he showed the projected payback to the business managers, the response he got was, "Those are soft costs." Steve only got buy-in by figuring out an end-around play, taking advantage of being in the food-processing industry, where the ability to launch a recall of defective products very rapidly can be crucial—

The way I finally sold the project was to show that it enabled a higher quality data capture in order to feed the product-recall database. Everyone agreed that being able to do product tracking and very rapid product recall was important. So important that they really didn't care if the project had a demonstrated payback or not, because the recall feature was like an opportunity cost payback.

So we sold the project on that basis. We went back three years later, after allowing enough time to get the technology fully absorbed, and were able to show that the warehouse had doubled the throughput with fewer people.

When we showed the benefits, that sparked a lot of other change. Once the people absorbed the base technology, then they got creative. Now that we can do this, and now that we know these things, we're in a different place to make decisions. The business added on a labor management and incentive pay system that would not have been possible without the new technology base, which greatly improved productivity.

So there wasn't much argument on its value. But it proved to be a great study to say that it's an enabler and not only of a better immediate business process, but as you know more about your business, you start reacting off of that and you'll come up with other ideas. You'll begin to make progress from a new base.

Experiences like that help our management team put more of a value today on the improvements that are made by further technology around a process. We have a much richer information base; and when you have that, the managers have more perspective and they'll make decisions that will continually add more value.

Still, even as a CFO, Steve Hankins frequently uses a measure of success that's different from other people's—

I talk a lot about how cost really isn't necessarily measured in head count, but instead taking the same number of people and enabling them to do more.

In an economy where so many jobs are being lost, that's a principle worth noting.

Budgeting for Success

Every division, workgroup, and other kind of unit in every company faces the regular challenge of how to divide up their monetary pie. For IT, those decisions can impact the entire organization. Jerry Gross put that into perspective—

How you spread your technology investments differs for each company depending upon its stage of maturity. So if you've got a company that is in a high growth industry and is fairly mature, then you may have 30 percent of your technology investments in just running the business, 40 percent of your investments in growing the business, and the rest of it in innovating.

This spread will also depend upon where the company is in its life cycle of technology, its use of technology, and what industry it's in.

At Washington Mutual we strive to set these limits in terms of the types of investment we're making, and we monitor the compliance with that on a quarterly basis. And that helps in prioritizing; you don't want to be putting everything into growing the business without making appropriate investments in the upkeep and the maintenance and support of underlying infrastructure. So there's no hard science here, but it does help in terms of prioritization across the portfolio.

At some companies, IT is expected to be self-sustaining. As noted earlier, that was true at Chevron, and remains true following the merger with Texaco. Dave Clementz explained, "I had to recover my costs from my internal customers. There are no allocations of the cost for IT. I had to go sell my services to the internal operating companies as if I had a shingle on the outside."

In fact, that arrangement was a result of Dave's own handiwork—

The business model [of IT] called for developing a portfolio of services that I offered to the business units and let them pay for directly, with no cost subsidies from one product line to another, and no corporation allocations.

Sometimes the CEO would be the customer for a particular piece. When we put in the digital backbone, he paid for a lot of the foundational work, the architectural design, some of the negotiations for the telecom circuits, and so forth. The corporation covered that up front working capital.

But I put in a very low cost, high performance global network and infrastructure—the digital railroad that connected all the operating companies. We ran that, but we charged a fee.

But Chevron IT made sure their internal customers were getting good value—

We do relentless benchmarking on our IT costs over and over and over again—by op code, by corporate, by whatever you can imagine.

We've done half a dozen studies in the past two years just prior to and during the merger, which we've shown to the executives. I'm able to say, 'By benchmark, I can tell you to the nearest tenth of a percent where we're at relative to the competition.' The benchmarking regularly shows we run at the bottom of IT costs for an enterprise our size. We run at about 0.8 percent of revenue; the industry average is 2 to 3 percent. And when you look at the infrastructure piece alone, we're at 0.4 percent for the digital infrastructure, and the industry averages 0.8 percent. So we tend to run at the bottom.

Now if you're out in Singapore or South Africa or somewhere and you see these studies, you say, 'Well, these don't really apply to me because I can get labor a lot cheaper out here,' or whatever. And that's fine and you can criticize them all you want. But no matter how you slice it and dice it, we are at the bottom. We are really at low cost, and I would say that we're delivering a pretty high value proposition for what people are getting for their money, because we've been able to drive standards. But if you can't drive standards, you can't drive high value at low cost.

Still, how does a business unit know they're not being overcharged by IT?

It's time we got everyone to start thinking of the IT investment they're making, and not just the on-going cost. If all you think about is the cost, then you're going to miss the opportunities. And some vendor will come along, take a look, and say, 'Oh, that's no problem, we can take that over for you.'

The idea of installing a process for making sure that IT expenditures line up with the company's strategic plan finds many enthusiasts, such as at CommonHealth, where, according to Craig Cuyar, "major IT expenditures are driven by a strategic plan. And in my humble opinion they should always be driven by a plan. That's how come the IT organization can manage enterprise expectations with a clear understanding of where they believe the organization needs to go."

Cuyar believes that "It's a paradoxical relationship, because when you deal with different business units, not all of them have a cohesive strategic plan. So when you try to align IT investment decisions with business strategy, it becomes difficult if you don't have a clear business strategy."

One problem, Craig suggests, arises when—for whatever reason—either the business planning isn't done well enough, or enough time isn't taken—

Most organizations I've been involved with are so focused on getting the job done, whatever the job might happen to be, that planning activities mostly take a back seat to production activities. So when it comes to building that comprehensive strategic plan, it's always the lowest priority on a long but distinguished list.

As a result, when you start to—I use the term tongue in cheek—'cobble together' a strategic plan, it's an activity that doesn't necessarily have everybody's undivided attention.

Rethinking the Role of the CIO

How IT is viewed by the business side depends heavily on how much clout the CIO has and how he is perceived by leadership. We've looked at an aspect of this earlier in these pages, but it has an important bearing on the issue of managing IT, as well. Some business leaders, such as Stan Hupfeld, are sensitive to the need because of the route they themselves took on their way to the top—

> I've been fortunate in having worked under two CIO's in my career. I don't consider myself skilled technologically. We have for some time now placed our CIO among the most senior managers that we have, and that individual reports directly to me. It's almost necessary that that individual report to me, unaided or unaffected by any other reporting relationships. It's just too major a piece of our business for me not to be involved and knowledgeable of it.
>
> [The change from the CIO as simply a department head to a direct report of the CEO] was heavily my decision. I think it's just partly understanding of what's going on in the industry, and partly because of the dollars involved.
>
> We used to go to the board of directors for authorizations, and even though we were asking for a lot of money, their eyes would begin to glaze over after a little while. And the eyes of the senior management glazed over. I think it just became clear to the industry and to us that, with what was at stake here, the CIO needed to be as senior a manager as your Chief Financial Officer—they need to have the same status in the organization.

The larger the organization, naturally, the more complex the nature of the CIO's role. At ChevronTexaco Dave Clementz was, before his retirement, wearing two hats—

> The ChevronTexaco Information Technology Company is a wholly owned subsidiary, run like a business. I had bottom line accountability for budget, I had to stay within that budget.
>
> To support the merger of Chevron with Texaco and Caltex, we divided the IT organization into two major chunks of activity. One was called the Embedded IT Groups, and their people managed most of what the operating companies did with their data and their own applications. So they would do local assistance for application support, for data management, and so on.

And then there was the Enterprise Group, the company that I was president of for six and a half years, which provided specific services that supplement the Embedded Groups. For example, we ran the financial systems and the HR systems for the corporation.

To govern the Enterprise Group, we had four people who were operating company CIOs. We had the CIO for North America Upstream—the finding and producing arm, a resources part; International Upstream; Global Downstream—meaning refining, marketing, retail and so on. And a CIO for all the corporate departments—HR, Finance, Treasury, Legal, you name it. The seven of us, with me at the head, constituted the Council of CIOs, and we met every Thursday for a minimum of an hour and a half.

For those CIOs, about 20 percent of their activity was focused toward the enterprise and 80 percent toward their individual operating units. Actually, it usually works out to be about 100 percent plus 20 percent—it's a tough job to live in the white space.

In addition, as the Enterprise CIO, my job was to be IT focused, with about 1,200 people in the central IT codes reporting to me, and about 2,100 IT people in the operating companies.

The CEO of Integris Health has his own way of describing the CIO's role in running IT, and it grows out of his experience as having been a CIO himself. Stan Hupfeld—

There are two kinds of CIOs and they're both necessary, and sometimes the same person can wear the two hats. To use a farming analogy, if you were a pioneer in America determined to settle into farming, first you had to find a spot and make sure the soil was fertile for the kinds of crops you wanted to grow. You had to stake it out and get the claim to the land. Then you had to clear the trees, pull up all the boulders, and get the roots out. All of that is what I call pathfinding. Then plow the furrows, prepare the land, plant the seeds, tend the crops day by day as they grow, until you're ready for the harvest. Back and forth behind your plow-horse, day after day, year after year.

This second part is the farming. For the CIO, much of the job is going up and down the rows, back and forth, year after year, making the crops grow and making them grow better.

I've always considered myself to be in the first category more than the second. I can do both, but I tire quickly of driving my tractor up and down the rows. And there's no path-finding involved. I get a little bit bored and frustrated.

Historically CIOs just drove up and down the rows. My predecessor was that way, and I think a lot of traditional IT folks get in that comfort zone and it's just hard to step out. For the pathfinding part, you're taking risks, introducing more complexity, getting up there in front of people and making promises—some of which you may not know how you're going to deliver on. And some people just aren't cut out for that.

To Be or Not To Be Standardized

As you might expect, the question of standards for technology throughout the enterprise proves to be a hot-button. The Army's Carla von Bernewitz commented that "everybody thinks the problem is that there's a lack of standards, but that's completely backwards. The problem isn't with not having standards, it's with having so many competing standards. You've got to pick one, and nobody ever wants to do that. Same thing here in the Army. We have so many different systems initiatives and transformation initiatives." (To which she added, "By the way, 'initiative' is a code word for an unfunded program.")

Elsewhere, a company may feel compelled to standardize simply because it's more financially responsible. That's the situation sometimes encountered at Integris Health, as CEO Stan Hupfeld explained:

> Every year when it comes to budget time, in order to restrain the growth and the IT budget, we usually budget based on rolling out new solutions to all of our fourteen sites at the same time.
>
> But then we get down to the short straws during the budget process when we're trying to find places to cut, and we take that timing for Places A, B, and C and move them back a year. So we wind up making budget in the short term, but we delay full implementation another year and wind up supporting two or three systems because we haven't made the conversion in all our sites.
>
> And what we finally figured out is that there is some short-term liability that we need to take on for the long-term greater

good. In other words, it might be that rather than postponing implementation across the system, we might be better served to go ahead and bite the bullet, and implement on a faster schedule so we save the maintenance cost of two or three systems that need to be supported.

Frankly, we were deluding ourselves for years and it took somebody to come in and say, 'Look, you ought to be operating one system for accounting, one for patient registration, and one for clinical, but you're operating six.' And the maintenance cost of operating those six systems was horrendous.

One other factor, as well: there's also a limit on how many different technology suppliers you want to be dealing with, because with each additional one comes more technical training that you need.

Jeff Cohen, the former CIO of JetBlue Airways, gives standardization as one of the main reasons the airline manages to spend so much less on technology than the competition. "You have no need for technicians and developers and all the rest to support other platforms." He believes that, for JetBlue at least, not being standardized "could have meant as much as 60 percent more staff."

But not everyone agrees that standardization is always the way to go. Washington Mutual's Jerry Gross—

For a highly commoditized service, like for example desktops, we don't look for a single provider in just, say, Dell or HP or IBM. We use more than one company, and might make demands like, "If you fail to meet these service levels, then we want greater discounts," which we might take in the form of consulting services or something like that.

Or we might put into the purchase agreement a clause that says, in effect, "We need to have the right, if you're not performing, to reduce the amount we're purchasing from you and give the business to someone else, without any penalty."

On the other hand, Jerry makes an exception to his own rule: "When you're talking about something like database software, then a single provider makes a great deal of sense." Good point: when any product becomes essentially a commodity and you can get essentially the same set of virtues from a competitor's product, you have the flexibility of taking your business elsewhere if one provider isn't meeting your standards. At ChevronTexaco, Dave Clementz sees standardization as bringing a synergistic aspect—

This is a pure example of what I consider to be a third-order effect. For example, we have this major new system being installed, a system handling transactions of billions of dollars of information a month, and so it can't be allowed to fail. Training started in October or November of last year [2002], the system went live on January 1, and within a matter of days, thousands of people were using it. There were very few failures, very few bugs. One morning I went over to the Crisis Management Center where they were following the operations live, and saw how smoothly it was working.

The experience impressed Dave once again with the benefit of standardizing—

What struck me was how quickly any problems could be solved. Somebody would say, 'This software doesn't keep track of enough decimal places in this element,' and within that same day, a fix was being pushed out to all the users over the network.

Six or seven years ago when we had a major install like that, if you had a bug like the decimal-point issue, you wrote the patch and then you sent an army of people down the hallways with diskettes to go to each machine to load the patch. And now you just put it out on the network.

Still, the problems with this installation weren't all small ones; one was huge—

Within the first ten days or so of when they looked at the receivables, they started seeing this big chunk of money that was hung up in the system. And of course you want to get your hands on the cash, you want those big receivables.

Three months later, there was something like $150 million hung up and they still hadn't figured out the problem. Finally they came up with the answer: a big flaw in the process. Sally never told Charlie he was supposed to clear this account, or whatever. The front end didn't know what the back end was doing.

That would not have been visible with the old system. But once we streamlined the process, totally digitizing it, and were managing it at the enterprise level, you can see it.

Outsourcing Good and Bad

You sometimes hear people say something like, "Let's outsource the utility but keep the strategic internal." That sounds fine—but the first day the e-mail system goes down when the CEO wants to send a message, it's IT he or she is going to be screaming at. Common-Health CIO Craig Cuyar says, "A lot of organizations today tend to outsource the utility function, but the paradox there is an IT organization is seen in the eyes of the end user as a collective organization. And if you can't deliver the utility services, you'll never be able to build a credible relationship with the business units sufficiently well to be seen as a partner capable of helping them meet their business objectives."

> I will liken it to Abraham Maslow's 'needs hierarchy'—you'll never reach self-actualization if you cannot meet basic needs. In an IT organization, you will never be able to demonstrate your ability to generate value for your organization if you cannot fulfill the need for basic services. For example, an IT organization cannot sell business units on their ability to drive value through the implementation of the latest technology if they cannot provide stable utility services like network connectivity, security, and e-mail services.
>
> When a frustrated end user calls the Help Desk to complain about their e-mail problems, they tend to connect their 'IT problem' to the 'IT staff'—regardless of whether they are outsourced or permanent employees of the organization. How can you convince this frustrated end user of the need to trust your IT organization with a multimillion dollar capital investment project, and the expected returns, when they just experienced dissatisfaction with the outsourced help desk staff? To the end-user community, the IT services are provided by a collective IT organization.

Craig believes this is an issue of reputation—whether IT can gain "the respect and the character" that has to exist in order to implement systems that will benefit both organizations.

And if IT outsources critical functions, what happens to innovation? Gary Moore, senior vice president of Cisco, has strong views on the subject—

> So you make a commitment: you'll let someone else run your data center, you'll let them run your network, at this price, for X years. All of a sudden, all the innovation is gone. It becomes an operational thing where you're just driving out costs versus trying to innovate.

Some well-known companies have outsourced their engineering to India. Cisco outsourced its manufacturing, but protects its engineering because we're a technology innovation company, which means we have to own engineering. I believe a lot of U.S. companies that have outsourced either engineering or the manufacture of some technologies are going to find that these elements really should be treated in a more proprietary way.

Elsewhere, though, others are having success with outsourcing certain of their IT functions. Dave Clementz—

We've outsourced a lot of the noncritical stuff—the mainframe is run by EDS, the network is run by EDS. It's just that you have this competency model and the level of the [in-house] customer's appetite for outsourcing. We're doing a study now to look offshore to lower the cost one more time and push some application maintenance out to India. With the merger came a data center in Manila—very high quality people, very high reliability. They've been doing all the SAP transaction support for parts of Finance and HR.

I tried very hard to set up flexibility so we could swing with the ebb and flow of demand. So when I'm hit with a hundred million dollar shortfall because the Chairman says no more discretionary IT projects, I can deal with it. I can make it go away in a hurry. I can reduce $100 million dollars in three months.

While you're pondering whether outsourcing IT functions is such a good idea, how about looking at whether IT could become a profit center? Among those subscribing to this idea is Washington Mutual's Jerry Gross:

One of the goals ultimately would be to monetize the IT function. That's easier said than done, because what can you monetize that isn't competitive advantage? I'm not sure we've figured that out yet. But it's a goal to turn technology into a profit center through deploying great technology into your back office and then looking at back-office functions and saying, 'Can I spin that off?'

Or in some cases, the front office. But we're like everybody, I think—struggling to determine whether we can spin off stuff that's providing us competitive advantage or cost leadership today, and generate revenues throughout the industry. We're still noodling through that.

If you look at the history of "Let's turn IT into its own business," the results are mixed. And more often than not, when I find a company that says they've done it, they've basically implemented a cost management system for IT, but the bulk of their clients are still the internal people. They haven't had much success going outside and generating new revenues for the company. When I offered this observation to Jerry, he responded—

> I think you're always going to have an uphill battle with your internal customers because they're going to say, 'We get priority, right?'
>
> I would have a hard time sitting in front of my board saying, 'Well, a core competency of ours is being an outsourcer.' They'd disagree and say, 'That would have us competing against EDS and IBM—what are you talking about!?'

IT and the Small Company

In many ways, East Industries' CEO David Wilson is a classic example of what you'd like to see most small business people take as an approach to technology. What drives this is not technology in itself, it's your business priorities.

You've designated someone on your staff to be in charge of technology, and teamed them with one or two outside consultants you've come to trust—people who have proven the ability to deliver by contributing ideas to let you take advantage of technology. People who can stay focused on the business reasons. David Wilson—

> Our IT guy is a very good long-term thinker, always ahead of the curve, even though I've always fussed at having to spend all the extra money on the technology side. But he seems to be right on target. I had pretty good faith in him initially and it's just grown.
>
> We are ahead of a lot of people. He understands our business. He manages it very well. And even though sometimes we say, 'Do we really need this, do we need to move up to this plateau, can't we just stay where we are?' I'll usually acquiesce and move up to the plateau, and then within two or three months we're all happy with the decision—it all makes sense. He has been a real inspiration in that area.

I reckon I'm not a technology whiz by any means, so I'm privileged to have somebody who can have enough insight to see what we need for managing our business in the way of emerging technology.

Like Dave, Keystone Marketing founder Karen Settle isn't big enough to do IT in-house—

I rely on consultants, and that includes two different programmers. One does our Internet training sites and our company website, and one does the programming site. The real key, and what makes the difference with these programmers versus other programmers I've interviewed or used, is they understand our business.

We run five Internet sites: Keystone University is an internal site that we use to train our people and update them on the products we represent and get them skilled. Keystone2000.com gives an overview of the company, for prospective clients. The third is the site our field people go to for filing their reports, that we use for analysis and payroll. And then we run two training sites for the sales reps.

The programmers will come to me and say something like, 'Karen, for your field reps, I'm wondering if you should port their reporting function to handhelds. Wouldn't it be a help to the reps to be in a retail store using a Handspring or a Palm to record the details of their visit, versus going home and doing it on their desktop computer?' And we are implementing this suggestion now.

Or because they're so in touch with our business, they will come to me and say, 'I read something about this new program,' or 'I came up with this idea for another client, do you think it's something you could use?' I can count on them.

Still, as much of a technology enthusiast as you might be, you can go too far the other way, to where technology becomes an end in itself. Dave Wilson—

We've had feelings a few times that we've been too technology driven and not business driven enough. And you can't let that happen. At times maybe we have been there, but we're trying to regroup and get back to basics.

[When the technology is right,] it gives you a level of confidence, so when you're with a customer you can pull up data immediately and provide them with all the answers to their desires and wishes of accountability, in any type of format they want. That keeps them happy and keeps them coming back to you.

For a company of any size, that's the name of the game, isn't it?

The question of how much of a budget to allocate for IT has always challenged even the best of small company managers. For a mid- or large-size company, at least there are published reference guidelines so you can be sure your decisions are within the realm of what other managers consider reasonable. For a small company, though, the answers may be a good deal tougher to come by. Eric Meslow of Timbercon sees this issue partly in terms of the company's bank balance—

If we net $6,000 one month, we have $6,000 to allocate to marketing, IT, product development, and so on. With such limited funds, it's very difficult to prioritize spending money on IT; some of the packages and software that we'd like to consider are expensive for a company our size. If we clear $50,000 in a year, we have $50,000 to allocate. IT alone could easily spend $100,000 in a year just trying to keep the computers up to speed and maintaining the best kind of servers, etc. With that, it's been a huge challenge to prioritize where the money goes.

Because some customers require us to utilize certain IT capabilities in order to do business with them, some of those decisions have been relatively easy to make, amortize, and show a return on investment. For the most part all those decisions have been very straightforward.

For example, we just had a requirement come up this week in which one of our largest customers has given us a scope of work that requires us to centralize and standardize around [a particular software package] for all of our communications with them. Within the scope of work this is not a 'We would like this,' it's a 'You must do this.'

Instead, we offered a more advanced solution with [a Microsoft product], and they're ecstatic. If we implement this solution, we will be doing something beyond any of their current suppliers.

So there's a leap-frogging type of situation going on with our customers. They say, 'We need this,' and we oftentimes give them something newer, better, or more advanced that allows them to say, 'Oh, that's kinda cool.'

That experience of a small company teaching technology advances to a larger customer is being duplicated elsewhere. Terry Szpak, founder of Telesystems West, has had the experience, as well—

We were working on a large project with a company, doing 120 locations for them, and we were trading files back and forth constantly [about the status of the project at each of the locations].

What we've done now is that we've posted the status of the job on line, so they know that at any point in time they can come visit us on line and see what's done, what needs to be done, if we're falling behind, or if we're ahead of the game. Instead of having to call, 'How's this going, how's that going?' they just visit online and look for themselves. They just love it because they're totally up to date on what we're doing.

Timbercon's Eric Meslow offered advice that works for any budget-sensitive small business—

I think the biggest thing that I would say to anybody running a small business is: don't overlook the technology side. You have to invest the money, you have to take the plunge. One of the areas that we've been very fortunate in is data back-up. We have gotten away without running tape or anything until recently.

That was a potentially catastrophic oversight, but it's a lot of money; it just boils down to money. You're a small business owner, you look at a data backup device that costs $9,000, and the software to run it costs $8,000. You're struggling to grow the company, and that's an employee for half a year that can maybe generate twice that amount of business. But you cannot afford to overlook the technology.

Karen Settle added her own advice about how a small company can get the best advantage of its technology dollars—

I look very closely at how technology will let the business run better and more efficiently. And it's how I keep my costs down, because I usually absorb the costs of the technology in a year or two and it helps me expand as well as, in all honesty, limit the number of people I need. We were able to get rid of one data analysis person, and I need fewer project managers or field managers because of everything that's now done on a technology basis.

I think that probably is the most important thing a company has to look at. If I was starting all over again, starting a business today, I would look first at how to use technology versus people. I might invest more up front in technology. And I would talk to a lot of people, talk to some competitors, see how they do it, talk to several programmers, look at magazine articles and books to see what other small companies are doing.

I think technology has been our strength, and anyone starting a business needs to look at that first. The way you do an org chart of people, you want to do an org chart of technology and how you'll use it.

Take-Aways

The "ruby slippers" approach to problem solving says that what you need may be staring you in the face. In earlier chapters, we've talked about the various roles of an effective CIO, the need for the CIO to sit at the table with top management, and about IT having a partnership role on any project with the business leader.

Beyond that, for me, what "ruby slippers" means in this context is that it's time company management became fully aware that IT has vastly more to offer than installing computers and hooking them up together. Sure, some companies have already made a good deal more headway with this than many others. In this chapter we heard about one company where "IT has evolved from being order takers, to advisors, to being key influencers, to being key decision makers."

But it's time—well past time, in fact—for all the laggard companies to figure out that the value of their IT department is being largely wasted, unless the technology folks are making major contributions in the perennial struggle to solve business problems and move the organization toward achieving its goals.

PART FOUR

Controversy and Miscellany

9

"Everything That Can Be Invented Has Already Been Invented"

> [Nicholas Carr's *HBR* article presents] a very dangerous message when taken out of context, because the basic information that he uses is correct but the things that people have put into the words that he's written I think can be very misleading.
>
> —Prof. Lee Schlenker, *University of Lyon*

In 1843, the head of the U.S. Patent Office, writing about the advancement of invention from year to year, commented that it "seems to presage the arrival of that period when human improvement must end." (That statement somehow transformed over time into the popularized version, the delightful-because-so-absurd phrase used as the title of this chapter.)

To some corporate and IT leaders, that *Harvard Business Review* article, one of a set of articles on technology, made as much sense as the mis-quoted version of the remark about the flow of inventions coming to an end.

The article was written by Nicholas Carr, a former *HBR* executive editor, and it made waves. That must have been Carr's intent, because the piece ran under the in-your-face title of "IT Doesn't Matter." He argues that IT is the most recent in a series of developments that changed the face of industry—the steam engine, the railroad, telegraph, telephone, electric generator, internal combustion engine. Each, he says, brought short-term advantage to forward-looking companies, but each in turn became a "commodity input." Once that happened, "From a strategic standpoint, they became invisible; they no longer mattered."

He then goes on to take the position that information technology today is for the most part at the end of the road in terms of its being able to be of real strategic value to a company. He argues that there is no competitive advantage to be gained from IT.

This will surprise some people and annoy others, but I agree with much of what Carr says. In fact, I find it quite easy to accept 70 or 80 percent of the reasoning in that article. How could there be any competitive advantage if you buy a commodity? A spreadsheet is a spreadsheet is a spreadsheet, right?.

But it's not the technology that gives advantage, especially in the longer term; it's how a particular company uses the technology. A truly innovative organization finds ways to use "commodity" technology in truly innovative ways. To cite the example of two companies mentioned more than once by those whose comments follow in this chapter, neither Dell nor Wal-Mart has any technology that their competitors can't also purchase and put to use. The advantage a particular company gets out of any process, product, or approach goes back to how well they can figure out clever, effective, differentiating ways to use it.

In doing the interviews for this book, we asked a number of people about that article—not just IT people but business people as well. What follows is a collection of responses.

Reactions Hot and Cold

Some people were enthusiastic in their support of Carr's proposition—at least of individual points, if not the whole thesis. Among them, Airborne's Rachelle Mileur—

> We do view the basic operation of some of our systems as a commodity. We need to be able to achieve highly available, highly reliable, highly performing systems and drive down that cost. Our network, our voice system, our infrastructure that backs up those systems are clearly commodities, and we need to get those as cost efficient as possible.
>
> To some extent, our core system of rating a shipment is a commodity in that we're not looking to continually improve. Everybody in this business needs to [rate shipments], and in a reliable manner. So we manage that with fairly thin staff.

So Rachelle accepts the notion that the infrastructure parts of IT belong in the commodity category. However, she doesn't stop there, adding that "This allows us to transfer some of the cost savings into areas that are certainly not a commodity, like our customer-facing, customer-touching systems."

Another view, from Professor Schlenker in Europe, also finds things to admire and others to condemn—

> On the one hand, it's a credit to *HBR* that they're able to focus so much attention around an article whose arguments are really fairly simple. I think the reactions to the article are extremely valuable and help position the worth of information technology today. Look at the wide range of people who responded in writing to the article, coming from different perspectives, from different industries, and actually from different intellectual slants.
>
> But there are several lessons that I think both the author and his critics would agree upon. IT is just a start. The competitive advantage comes from what you do with it. Companies have been spending a lot of money without really understanding the business reason or rationale behind it. Where I would totally agree with Nicolas Carr is that we need to understand what the business objectives are, and develop an ROI that helps us focus on where we're going.
>
> The major criticism would be that it's a very dangerous message when taken out of context, because the basic premise that he puts forward is valuable but the things that people have put into the words that he's written, I think, can be very misleading.
>
> Take the assertion that information technology is a commodity. When you look the incremental versus the strategic advantages that your company can derive from IT, you see how IT can serve as building blocks of business value.
>
> IT's major advantages today aren't necessarily in the computing power, but that we're now applying technology to different aspects of the business. We're beginning to apply it to process-centric systems, and now to collaboration. That's not a difference in degree, it's a difference in kind.

The reaction from Tyson Foods' CFO Steve Hankins was typical of many; he commented, "That was not the most informed or well researched article I've ever read." When we mentioned the piece to CommonHealth's Craig Cuyar, he noted, "I actually have it sitting on my desk," and then proceeded to share his views—

Nicholas Carr assumes that we have learned all that we can about the world of IT. More specifically, he doesn't consider the broad definition of 'technology.' Technology has to do not with the bits and the bytes of hardware and software, but with the practical application of knowledge and how you apply it.

But if technology is understood to be a practical application of knowledge, then my basic response to the article is that the body of knowledge is constantly growing. We're always learning. Every day is an opportunity to learn new things, apply new ideas, and develop that body of knowledge. Carr's analogical references to the commoditization of railroads and electrical power grids lose sight of the fact that there is more to Information Technology than just the deployment, support and maintenance of the infrastructure. There will always be a new way of thinking about and 'applying our knowledge' to the world of Information Technology. The argument that we have learned everything that we can about IT is posited incorrectly.

Clearly we haven't learned all that we could learn. But one thing in this we can all agree on is that technology will continue to change significantly. And there will always be other opportunities to uniquely apply that knowledge to your organization, to your clients, and to produce competitive advantage in your respective industry.For example, recent advancements in storage and digital asset management practices are revolutionizing the way we work in the advertising industry. New media software applications are enabling a whole new community of workers to develop content beyond just desktop publishing and static images. If we all agreed that IT didn't matter and was completely commoditized, we wouldn't be able to provide business value and competitive advantage through the application of these technologies.

The idea that we're at the end of the road for technology innovation is a bizarre concept to get your arms around. It's like saying that we've learned all we're going to learn. I'm not sure there's anything on earth about which that can be accurately claimed.

ChevronTexaco's Dave Clementz found the article "very provocative," and commented, "I would agree with the author on many points—the technology itself is not a differentiator." But the same doesn't hold true, Dave insists, when what you're talking is how the technology is used. "It's the application of the technology that's always been the differentiator," he argued. "Carr's thesis assumes that everybody takes advantage of the technology that's in front of them at the time. Of course, it doesn't happen like that."

This doesn't mean that Dave takes exception with the article's main argument. On the contrary—

> In general, I agree with the author. I believe that the technology itself has no value until it finds its place in our business processes. And that the title of the article, 'IT Doesn't Matter,' is true.
>
> That's a provocative question, does IT matter? And it doesn't, if you're not going to take advantage of what it offers and change the business model. This is really about enabling a new business model. It's not about installing technology.
>
> In the oil industry, that's not a new argument. We're a $100 billion revenue company and we only have 50,000 employees. So what's going on here? We have anywhere from about 100,000 to 200,000 contractors supporting us year upon year. Now these contractors are available to anyone. The technology they use to drill wells is familiar throughout the world. People can poke holes in the ground anywhere they want, even including 7,000 feet below the surface of the water in the Gulf of Mexico, where we've just had a major discovery.
>
> Some people discover oil and some don't, but the technology is available to everybody. The raw, hard-iron technology to build a refinery, to drill a well, to lay down a pipeline is the same for everybody. The seismic technology is the same. The equations you write down to look at the reflections off the earth are the same. It's just that some people rewrite the equations, and they restudy the map based upon what they see in that particular environment.
>
> It's not hard for guys in our industry to relate to the concept that it isn't about the technology. Some of my friends in the Chevron IT company got all upset when that article came out, and some said, 'This is slam-on garbage.' And I just totally disagree. Nike makes shoes in a way that nobody else makes them and they have a marketing scheme that sets them apart. Anybody can do this. But why don't they? And why don't they make the same amount of money? Why are there only three major oil companies left on the Fortune 100 today when there were 25 when I joined the company 30 years? It's not the technology; some people just do it better.

Competitive Advantage

People we spoke to were lining up to refute the idea that technology can't be used as a tool for gaining competitive advantage. We found wide agreement that this does indeed describe the situation in many companies, usually accompanied by what amounted to a "but if." Jerry Gross put it this way: "Technology as a competitive advantage is only realized if it's embedded within the customer product. Carr's view misses the point. The bulk of the competitive advantage comes through how the organization *uses* the technology."

Jerry added, "In my view, he was too focused on technology and he didn't focus on the people or the processes. Here's the thing: sometimes the best use of technology is in ways it was never intended to be used."

Mary Kay's Kregg Jodie felt that "The article was suggesting that everybody's got basically the same packages, and so how can that be strategic?" Kregg insisted, "There are a lot of alternatives beyond just having the packages. If you're developing technology inexpensively and you're applying it directly to an enabled strategic plan, then it can have huge payoff. And also," he said, "as technology continues to change, that leads to opportunities to do things differently." Precisely. Using technology to do things differently provides the leverage of gaining an advantage, even if only temporary.

Steve Hankins offered a different explanation of a reason for disputing Carr's thesis—

> Technology is an enabler. I know I probably sound like everybody's cookbook on this, but I fundamentally believe that a lot of people still don't get that what we're really talking about here is the process and how you enable the process.
>
> When you go back to the question of 'does IT really matter,' [Carr] says everybody has the same stuff. I would disagree with that because if everybody had the same stuff, at least out in the retail business, we'd all be like Wal-Mart. And everyone is not like Wal-Mart. There are companies totally struggling with a lot of things that Wal-Mart does quite easily.
>
> Take SAP, for example. People start slamming SAP and they really never realize that they're not in a computer project, they're in a business process reengineering project. And if you miss that, then there's a good chance you're going to fail, you're going to screw up your world.

And even if all the top companies have SAP, that software has so many of what I call knobs and buttons and switches to throw to arrive at your company's configuration that I doubt if any two installations look alike. So it's process again.

I look across a large portfolio of companies out there and see huge differences in technology capability.

Dave Clementz was another of the several who cited Wal-Mart to refute the thesis of Carr's article. "Wal-Mart is the number one company in the world not because of the technology they use to enable their supply chain. It's because they thought through the business model that puts most of the costs of the distribution and the supply of their products on somebody else. They thought it through and they relentlessly worked to refine that model year after year."

Ditto GMAC-RFC's Greenwood—

I've drawn a chart up for my executives—I put on the left side the business domain knowledge, and on the right side I put the IT domain knowledge. I start with the IT side, where we know the most—the business doesn't really know anything about infrastructure, operations, network operating systems, and so on.

The very far left is business intimate domain knowledge—it could be hedging factors, securities, risk management around credit, consumer or asset, or product criteria, or business rules that are related to how you make a product. But as you keep progressively going to the left and you start putting applied technology to the business intimacy that you need, that's where you get the real value.

On the other side, that's where the commodity part is. But it's when you apply technology to the business intimacy—that's when you get the value.

When you sit down and talk to your CEO, suppose you've gone from 99.1 percent availability to 99.5 percent availability, do you send shivers up and down his spine about how well you invested that money? Not at all.

But when you go to him about a success on the other side, he may say, 'This new product introduction you've done has increased our competitive position and improved revenues substantially.' And they go jumping up and down. That's where they get the excitement. And that's where you get the competitive advantage.

Technology for Employees

Another area of objection to Carr's thesis had to do with how new technology benefits employees. ChevronTexaco CIO Dave Clementz—

> When our employees got their new PCs with all this horsepower, they were just absolutely ecstatic. Talk about productivity push, their productivity just soared. We took notice of the things that happened in the first wave and decided that, instead of waiting for it to happen with time, we were going to speed up the deployment.
>
> We changed the old website where you go to get information about the desktop, to a productivity-push website where people can leave messages, they can chat, they can share best-practices. People go up and say, 'Here's what I learned today, did you know you can do this and that?' and so forth. And they can post questions. So there's this website out there that's become very active. It just went live in early July but it's taking off, it's growing exponentially. People are excited.
>
> One thing that wasn't mentioned [in Carr's article] was what do we need to do to effect change in the culture of an organization. When we identify the problem sufficiently well enough so that people begin to take notice, they catch on quickly and they say, 'Yes, this makes perfect sense.'

Earlier in these pages, the co-founder of Telesystems West, Terry Szpak, described how his company is using its own Voice over IP technology to cut down on the commuting time of their employees and avoid the need for the field people to stop by the office each morning and evening to pick up assignments and turn in worksheets. His further comments on the subject bear on the present issue—

> We have one part-time worker who used to have commute from Kent to Bellevue. On a good day it was about an hour's drive. For a half a day of work, it just seemed like it wasn't worth it for her and she was debating what to do.
>
> She's such a great employee that we didn't want to lose her. We put an Internet phone in her home and now she works from there. She goes on the Web and accesses the information from the calendars that the guys use, and does her billing for us, all remotely so she doesn't have to commute any more. She has saved herself two hours a day of fighting traffic.

Sure, the competition will probably catch on in time, erasing the edge; but until that happens, Telesystems has gained a clear advantage.

Technology For Customers and Vendors

Nobody would argue against the view that serving customers better than your competitors is one rung on the ladder of competitive advantage. In Steve Hankin's view, staying in the forefront of technology makes that possible, and he, too, cites the Wal-Mart case:

> I jokingly say sometimes there's a difference between having an education and using an education. There's a great variation in how people use technology and how effective they are. There are no secrets at Wal-Mart. Everything they do can be found in a process map and a lot of it you can just draw yourself pretty quickly after talking to them.
>
> So there's no great mystery to all that. So why can't everybody be Wal-Mart? There's all types of issues along the way, not to mention the fact that Wal-Mart grew up from a little pup to a big dog. A lot of these other companies grew to be a kennel of dogs. You know, they bought this and bought that and bought the other thing, putting businesses together, and now they're a really big company, but all those pieces are separate. And they come to you and say, 'We want to do common buying across all these entities and we want to communicate with you electronically.' And their entities can't even communicate electronically with each other, much less bundle that all together to communicate with us.
>
> So I don't see that everybody has the same technology base. They may have the same names, the same gadgets, but I don't see a world where everybody is now at a baseline, so it doesn't make any difference anymore. It hasn't come to that.

Dell offers another classic example. Supposedly it was easy to copy them. Even powerhouses like Hewlett-Packard are still trying to figure it out, having a hell of a time trying to emulate them, and have not been able to.

Yes, it's technology, but it's also process, and none of that is patentable. The competitors have even hired people who worked for Dell, and they still can't get in the same game. Dell just seems to be able to constantly stay one step ahead. During a period of massive slowdown in the last two or three years, they have gained market share by double digits, driving the IBM's and the HP's crazy.

You can't readily take existing processes that you've accumulated over time, and retrofit a Wal-Mart model or a Dell model back on top of them. Still, in the view of Lawrence Baxter, "We're probably at a classic intersection of the road."

> I think there are a lot of enigmatic and almost contradictory attitudes. On any given day, I think many business leaders, and even some IT leaders, would agree with that article. That is to say, IT is no longer a strategy by itself; it's something that should be seen and not heard, to use the old Victorian phrase about children. Today users want it to be reliable and available, basically to just stay in the background. We'll just pay for somebody to keep it out there.
>
> On other days those very same people may say technology is not responsive enough. 'We want these people to be accountable to us because we're finding that we can't be flexible enough in our businesses if we don't get quicker response and reliability, and good cost effectiveness from IT.'
>
> So when the controversy broke out about that article, I could see both sides of the case right away. The general mood for the business folks here is, We like what we see—very tight discipline, with enterprise-wide control and leverage.

They like that because it means that IT doesn't get into trouble. But that's the part everyone wants to take for granted. Lawrence fingered a key flaw in Carr's argument with his remark that people on the business side complain about not being flexible enough if they can't get quick, reliable response from IT. Business people want IT as a partner, not just as a group that keeps the candles lighted.

Infrastructure Spend vs. Competitive Spend

If you think about the IT investments that you're making today, roughly what percentage are things you have to do to stay in the game versus things that you believe might differentiate you from your competitors? A couple of answers, first from Roger Smith—

> Probably 80/20—meaning 80 percent infrastructure and 20 percent cutting edge. It's difficult to come up with a definitive

split because, being a large company, our infrastructure is pretty vigorous, so what may be infrastructure to us might be cutting edge to another company.

Now, that is a fascinating notion: what looks like technology infrastructure to a giant, global company could seem like a differentiator somewhere else. The implications seem to me well worth pondering. Roger continued—

Also, we can take advantage of some of the technology our holding company has in place.

I don't think our [in-house] clients know the value of handling the mechanics correctly. Take the costs for firewall or anti-virus. Before I became involved in technology governance, I would have had no idea what the annual cost of this was to the firm. I would just expect it to work. We tell colleagues that technology enables us to filter spam, for example, and they say, 'That's great.' It's a twenty-second conversation.

What counts more to our clients and colleagues are things like collaboration strategy. That's the space that we invest in today: knowledge management, information management, and collaboration.

Even so, Roger gave a vote to Nicholas Carr in the way he ended this comment: "None of that is going to give us an edge per se, it's just that's probably where that 20 percent spend will be.'

Jerry Gross also sounded in on the same topic—

When I read that article I thought, 'Here's a guy who's looking at the cost it takes to put in a new network or the cost to buy a new PC.' Of course, a PC for the sake of a PC is very hard to understand in terms of return on investment.

When we measure the success of a project, it's the people, the process, and the technology. Most companies are just focused on the technology—'I spent $100 million to implement this technology. What did I get for it?'

No, no, no. You spent $100 million on technology, you spent maybe $30 million or $50 million on new processes and new work flows, and maybe you spent another $20 million on training programs to change the behavior of your employees.

So if you look at technology just for what's seen, that's a sliver of the technology investment. I think there are very few technologies just on their own where there's a return on investment. There's got to be a change in behavior, whether it's employee behavior, or customer behavior.

And that's what we're trying to tap into in our metrics. For example, when we put in Instant Messaging, we said, 'We believe there is value in employees changing the employees' behavior with the use of Instant Messaging.'

And so we sat down and said, 'Okay, what are the possible behavioral changes that could occur using IM across the enterprise?' And, including input from our employees, we came up with what we believe were the benefits associated with that—including better customer service and better employee enabling.

Here's another good example of the "unexpected benefits" mentioned above—

We were surprised to find that IM was actually a better e-learning tool than any standard e-learning you put on the Internet. Somebody who's having a problem doing something on his computer will IM a request, and somebody else will take the time to walk him through.

We recognize right up front that technology for the sake of technology is not enough. It's behavioral change and it's process change that matters.

Take-Aways

Any piece of writing that can generate as much heat and storm as the Carr article stands as a compliment to the author, and provides a valuable service by stimulating argument and discussion. Nicholas Carr may be off base in terms of some of his conclusions…but our hats are off to him nonetheless.

There was quite a reaction at Microsoft to the article, some of it on the order of "this is horrible, I disagree with all of it." For myself, I agree with a good part of what he has to say. I agree 100 percent that the primary issue is the application of technology, not technology as an end in itself.

The infrastructure part of IT may not be very thrilling, but any business leader who ignores the contributions that technology can make to helping the company achieve its strategic goals is headed for trouble. It doesn't matter that the same technology is available to everyone else; as pointed out repeatedly in the above, it's not the technology per se, but how the organization uses it. And whether the organization is willing to face the need for culture changes that allow it to take full advantage of the benefits that the technology can bring.

Carr's article does do a service, though, with the implicit reminder about insuring that your IT expenditures are worthwhile and bringing real benefits—which is an argument in favor of the kind of follow-up audit we call for in Chapter 5.

The article also serves to remind us of the fundamental importance in maintaining management engagement and oversight in all aspects of technology use in the company. The fact that this could still be a subject of debate suggests that management has not been very intimately engaged. And the senior executives we talked to for this book, while agreeing with the bulk of the article, certainly felt that they saw ways to innovate with technology. Unless IT becomes core to the business, the risks are very real that some of Carr's conclusions will actually come to pass. It's going to take the personal engagement of business leadership to make sure that doesn't happen.

But in companies able to add the ingredient of innovation, technology evolution can lead to dramatic changes and bring significant advantage. And that's where technology becomes exciting.

The advances in technology through the nineties gives a suggestion of what's to come in this decade. As many have said, including Microsoft Chairman Bill Gates, the evolution of technology in the next ten years will be more dramatic than in the last ten.

So my response to Nicholas Carr is: you've done everyone a service by raising these issues, but I and many others disagree with some of your conclusions and final advice.

10

...And in Conclusion: A Collection of Other Ideas and Viewpoints

> We want to be able to use technology to support the process we designed, rather than letting technology enable us to continue bad processes. That turns out to be a very hard thing to do.
>
> —Dr. Patty Gabow

In the course of doing the interviews for this book, Bill Simon and I encountered a remarkable number of intriguing stories, worthy ideas, valuable suggestions, and revealing personal experiences that didn't fit into any of the earlier chapters, but that we felt we would be remiss not to share. Here's a selection.

A Problem of Time

Wachovia's Lawrence Baxter sounded a rallying cry—for large companies, at least—by highlighting a pressing concern that is too often overlooked—

One of the things that I've felt myself under growing pressure on, and I'm sure it's common with most other people in my situation, is that the shear dynamics of business daily practice have a tendency to crush the amount of time you have for thinking and reading and really looking outside. And so what happened in the period during a recent merger we went through is that things like PDAs and cell phones were becoming mass-market items. I looked back to the last time that I was really able to think much about it, and at that point they were just early-adopter devices.

Meantime, our business grew to the scale where we've got a much larger number of customers and daily customer escalations and daily operational issues. Every code change involves an enormous testing and risk management.

I just literally lost touch with what was happening out in the real world, as it were. And I worry about that. It's a little bit like [Harvard Business School Professor] Clayton Christensen's point that large companies simply had the hardest time being able to even cope with any kind of innovation because it's antithetical to the dynamic by which they are driven.

Technology and Education: the Interactive University Story

Some years ago, the subject of online education at the college level stirred up quite a bit of controversy. Some college professors were taking the position that if a school offered degrees through online education, that school should have its accreditation lifted.

Not long after that flap, I had a speech to give at the University of North Carolina at Greensboro to an audience of professors and administrators. I got aggressive about saying this was the biggest example of a body of professionals sticking their head in the sand and running for cover to protect their own butts that I had ever seen. It promised to do the most damage possible to their most important person, the student. And it grew out of nothing more than professors fearing that online access to education would eventually detract from the need for their services, or somehow impede their ability to increase their income.

That effort of denying accreditation didn't win out in the end, and one of the finest, most successful universities in the U.S. today is a publicly held institution that's a leader in this—the University of Phoenix.

I still see some of the same kind of disgruntled mumblings on many college campuses. And while I also see signs of people on the campus opening up to the importance of technology at a strategic level, it's still frustrating to me that one of the most important segments of any society, education, continues to be viewed by too many people as having the least potential for benefits from technology and the Internet.

So I was heartened when the research for this book turned up an exemplary program combining education and technology. This one is called the Interactive University and originates from, of all places, Scotland. The COO is David Farquhar—

Professor Clayton M. Christenson has written that productivity in education will barely rise in the next five years. But personal interaction is the core. There is a complete misperception that you are either teaching face-to-face with human interaction, or you're doing it with computers.

Our premise is based on bringing these two together, combining the best of human interaction with the efficiency and reliability of Information Technology. Human interaction is best for motivating and for providing the context for learning, whereas technology can deliver access to knowledge and elements of automated assessment. That's our thesis.

This allows the education process to be distributed across both space and time, giving students more flexibility on where and when they study. The distributed education model can also be used to deliver education globally, with awarding institutions providing the content and assessment, and local educational institutions providing the context in the form of local tutoring and infrastructure.

Remote students see the same lectures by the course professor that the classroom students attend in person. Except that the remote students don't have to show up on the campus at the University of Glasgow at 8 a.m. every Tuesday and Thursday; they can download the lecture from the Internet and watch at their convenience. Periodically, the professor is available live on line to answer questions from the remote students.

The CEO of Interactive University, Professor Roy Leitch, commented that "We see technology as a catalyst for change—a change of working practices that improves the whole educational process."

The way that we set about convincing people of this was by demonstrating that it could be done in a professional, sustainable way. We convinced administrators to make the shift by saying, 'Invest up front in the development of interactive knowledge, get that going, and then display it to professors within the university.'

Now the same methods are being used even for the students on campus—

In five years, Heriot-Watt University [in Edinburgh, Scotland], where we began, moved to the point where about 40 percent of its whole delivery of on-campus education is done using these methods. That's a huge achievement.

We're hoping to take the program national, reusing the same content for a much wider range of students. Essentially we're the publisher and distributor for e-learning to all the colleges and the universities of Scottish higher education.

One of the reasons that our Scholar program has been so successful is that, just like any other change process, we started with defining very clearly where we were going. One of the reasons that educational solutions have not been successful in the past is because they have not begun by reengineering the educational process.

The Interactive University program has also been working with high-school level disenfranchised students, whose challenges are comparable to the inner city young people of the U.S. Again, David Farquhar—

We're reaching those disenfranchised students—100 percent of the market in Scotland now uses the program. All of the assessments that have been done show statistics that are amazing. The failure rates have fallen from 16 percent to 8 percent. The usage rate on this system has now gone up by one-third, because the students keep using it on their own time in the evening.

So what's our competition? Our competition is soap operas, our competition is MTV.

The ultimate measure is how well the students learn. At the university level, the founders of IU are ready to take a bow—

At the last exam period, we found that the results through our partner in Hong Kong were better than the students who were actually studying the same subjects on campus here. So where the student is accessing the content from and the way it's delivered is not what's important.

What's important, in other words, is the content, and how good a job people like Interactive University can do in designing the right delivery technologies. Personally, I say, 'Hurray.'

An Unexpected Observation

At first glance, you might expect that a technology project would flow much more smoothly when the business folks pushing it have a strong understanding of technology. Surprisingly, this can turn out to be a mixed blessing. Or worse.

Roger Smith explained the issue this way—

In many of these committee meetings [on a technology development project], one of the challenges we have only happens when the business people we've called on to take part in the process—the actual insurance professionals—are people who have an interest in technology. When you're in a meeting with them, they might say, 'Oh, yeah, if you gave this to me, I would do these three things with it.'

In Roger's view, that's when the alarm bells should start going off—

We have to step back and say, 'Okay, what would a person who *doesn't* have your technology skills or enthusiasm for technology do with that application?' With 38,000-plus employees, you can imagine the range [of technological sophistication]. You have to ask, 'What's the skill level, what's the aptitude, what's the interest of (or resistance by) the non-technical user going to be when they're given this application?'

In fact, it is almost a given that when populating a working group to discuss a technology solution, you do not get the colleagues who are technologically challenged. These folks are definitely not in the room—but they may be among possible users.

We try to avoid the 'If you build it, they will come' value proposition. So we spend some time on doing the 80/20 analysis. 'We hear 80 percent of the colleagues will use this the minute it's installed because they absolutely have to have it. Great,' we say, 'tell us about the other 20 percent.'

Or is that really 50 percent of people who won't see the value or won't want to take time to learn how to use the new whatever? So are we building it for people who would find a way to do the same thing anyway, or should we be building it for everyone in the user group? That's really where the process analysis comes in.

We all have to renew our driver's license every so many years, and the day it expires, we are out of compliance. So someone on the business side says, 'We have to do this, we can't avoid it; whether you give us technology or not, we have to do this.' The project gets approved and funded. And then when we start working, we need to ask, 'How will colleagues migrate to this? Readily? Readily because they have to? Or readily because they want to? Or not so readily at all?'

On the subject of how a new technology project gets started at Marsh, Roger explained—

Obviously the Holy Grail is to reduce handoffs, reduce steps, reduce re-keying, reduce multiple re-entry.

One example is a suggestion from the technology side. Technology colleagues in our company become aware of new developments that could lead to economies or efficiencies, or they recognize existing technology applications in the company that could be improved, and they suggest changes.

Another would be our firm's business leaders looking for a better way to deliver solutions to customers, a better way to give advice, or do something on the Web—that type of thing.

From GMAC-RFC's Rick Greenwood, a series of lessons based on hard experience—

The more intimacy you can build into your business knowledge, the higher the value you can achieve. Understanding the value proposition is absolutely number one.

The number two thing is having a discipline in the process—scoping the project, evaluating the requirements, and then deciding on how you're going to measure success.

The third aspect is that you've got to measure, measure, measure.

Another key element, the part that we actually are becoming more disciplined on, is defining the requirements. When you make people go through all the analysis and the requirements in getting a better definition, you start getting a much better cost/benefit analysis.

We've become pretty strict in holding people accountable. And we can show that those projects are plus or minus 20 to 40 percent of our projections. Any project that is not, is more likely to be plus or minus 400 percent; those are pretty startling numbers. I think if you check other CIOs who have gathered that information, you would find something like the same.

It used to take anywhere from twenty-one to twenty-seven days to fund a loan. We now have turned that around, and it's now three days. So we've eliminated twenty-four days.

Thoughts on reliability and security from the CIO of ChevronTexaco—

Before the merger with Texaco, the use of the internal network traffic was increasing 50 percent a year. The Internet part of that was increasing at 200 percent a year. As people were becoming more reliant on the network, then the reliability has to go up along with it, so we worked really hard on reliability.

I attended a conference, two days of CIOs getting together to talk about security. Everybody is facing the same problem. A lot of this has to do with how well your corporate people are trained. We have a whole issue around authorities in the SAP environment; we have too many administrators, and too many people have access to too many things. We've tightened that up a lot.

But also, we hire ethical hackers through our financial auditing firm, and their job is to see how fast they can break into the network—not if they can, but how fast they can do it. And every time I've run one of these, they get in, no matter how secure you are. Some of it takes them a while, using nefarious routes. Maybe they'll call up someone, give a plausible story, and ask for his password, and the person gives it to him.

(This approach, called "social engineering," is the subject of a book by co-author Bill Simon, called *The Art of Deception*. The book was written with renowned computer hacker Kevin Mitnick. As one of those reformed-hacker experts of the kind that Dave Clementz uses so effectively, Kevin runs a company called Defensive Thinking.com, providing security checks for major corporations and agencies in the U.S. and Europe.)

When I first came to this job, we ran a penetration audit and it was a disaster. This guy set up in a hotel room across from

Chevron Park and within two days had mapped out the entire network—from a hotel room, using the telephone. We started training people how to make real passwords; we found we had people using 'password' as a password, or 'secret,' or their own name.

We had a systems administrator in France—guess what he used for his password: 'system administrator.' How long did it take our penetration expert to figure that one out!

We closed most of those gaps and started requiring dual authentication using SecureID. But we did have one wake-up call—a worm that attacked the servers. We had a lot of servers that were not on what we call our shared server environment. They're not in a secure area where we can monitor them and make sure that all the patches are put on as soon as they arrive. They're underneath somebody's desk, or over by the Xerox machine. A lot of those didn't have the patches, and you couldn't get to them over the network.

So we have the hackers set up shop and break in under supervision, and sometimes we tell the people they're coming and sometimes we don't. And I will tell the hackers some of the high risk areas; I'll say, 'Don't waste your time over here; if you can get in, fine, but it doesn't matter, there's not too much there. But over here, they've been very recalcitrant lately and they think they've got their things locked down, and they don't want to have anything to do with enterprise standards. So this time go and see if you can do anything with them.'

I've had some interesting experiences with those kinds of recalcitrant customers. When you get within a few keystrokes of shutting down a refinery, they don't believe you and you tell them just how you're going to do it. And they say, 'Ah, s___— how'd that happen?'

From the World of Medicine to the World of Business

How likely is it that a field as specialized as "genomics information" would be developing methodologies that could prove useful in the hard-driving, competitive world of business? It may sound unlikely to you and to me, but not to a doctor, businessman, and technologist by the name of John Rootenberg—

We all suffer at times with a medical episode or event like a flu, or a series of strokes, or chronic condition like hypertension, osteoporosis, or arthritis—which occur over a short time, or over months or years. But there has never been a practical way for a physician or medical service to evaluate the interrelationship between the occurrences of these episodes over time. The best we've been able to do is merely answer by saying 'What happened?' The time has come to move on beyond that level of proficiency, and that's when IT is called in. Today the healthcare and life sciences industries have the opportunity to collaboratively answer the question, 'Why did this happen?' That's now becoming possible.

At the University of California, San Francisco, we're using large scale data warehouses for the integration and federation of disparate data types from a variety of sources, and applying advanced analytic tools, including neural networks. So we're building what we call the Clinical and Genomics Information Management System. With it, we're finally able to start interpreting the signs and symptoms of disease against the specific genetic constitution of individual patients.

Our preliminary results show that some current concepts of specific diseases will be challenged. For example, what was once thought to be a very specific disease might, in fact, be three distinct yet related disease entities. And we now think it's likely that patients with the same disease will be treated differently. The potential to use genetic and other information to determine which treatment will work best for which specific patient is called 'personalized medicine.' The ability to capture both the clinical expression of the disease and the genetic constitution of individuals, and then combine them, will ultimately provide a context for understanding the molecular basis of disease.

John anticipates that this capture-and-combine approach will become a powerful tool for business, as well—

I see the work we're doing at UCSF as very similar to situations faced by marketing-driven organizations trying to build customer-centric systems that move beyond the usual kind of single-business transaction histories. Why not a 'holistic view' of the customer?

Companies with multiple business units need to aggregate the data across the units. For example, a corporation might have a business unit that deals with an individual in their work setting and another unit that deals with the same customer in their home setting.

It might seem like combining these transactional perspectives would help predict future purchasing behavior, but it's not as simple as that. They'll need to develop contextual frameworks for interpreting and understanding why someone makes a purchase at a particular point in time, and why he or she decides on one product over another.

Without the ability to represent context and analyze results against a contextual backdrop, behavior will never truly be understandable or predictable. Businesses need to create a technology-mediated way of capturing and understanding the context of decisions. Only then will businesses be able to identify and keep current best customers, shed or limit their investment in those who will never become best customers, and convert those who have the potential to become best customers.

In the years ahead, I expect we'll see advancements from unlikely fields being brought into business, just as Dr. Rootenberg forecasts for the work his organization is doing in the field of medicine.

Corporate Technology in a Climate of Tight Budgets

How can IT adapt to a tough economic climate? Jerry Gross offered one answer: ease the pain by sharing it—

As an IT organization in any company today, not only are you under scrutiny, but you *should* be under scrutiny because most of your organization's expenditures are in people and technology.

Also, we're constantly looking at our business partners to be more accountable. So what you're seeing in these economic times are shorter-term deals. The days of five- and ten-year contracts are gone. Holding our vendors accountable to twelve-month contracts with service-level requirements and no termination penalties, these things are now standard. So are terms and conditions in contracts that if vendors run into fiscal difficulty, we have step-in rights.

Because of the economy, all of these things are changing the way we interact with our business partners, as well as how we manage our own technology business. These are now becoming standard in our contracts and in our agreements.

For Archie Kane, tight belts mean the need for tighter discipline within IT—

> The fact is that [in mid-2003] we've got a tough industry environment backed by a market that is still down. I grant you it has come back a bit, but it ain't going to rocket back to where it was two or three years ago. We'll see continued pressure on costs, continued pressure on margins, heightened consumerism, masses of more interventionist regulation. And we have to be able to respond to all of that and still make a buck.
>
> So I see IT becoming even more of a discipline. Your ability to have good financial management in a company now is kind of a prerequisite. If you ain't got it, you ain't going to survive.
>
> It's moving toward that; we're not quite there yet. But if you aren't competent about the deployment of IT as part of your overall business strategy and capability, you're not going to survive. So it's becoming a core competence of any business, particularly a financial business.

Rather than seeing IT as a competitive advantage, Archie sees it much more as "a vital ingredient in the core competence that you need to capture and leverage as part of your overall strategic competencies."

> People used to act as if, 'Oh, technology is just going to be a thing that in one great leap is going to allow you to become free.' I think that was a millennium-type thought. We're all moving away from that.

Process

Archie Kane again, this time reiterating a point made earlier by someone else—advice on fixing the processes before applying new technology; the repetition stands as a good reminder—

> You don't throw technology at existing processes. You need to take a real end-to-end view: sit and think about how you want to reengineer the whole thing and then apply good technology to it.
>
> We've made significant improvements in productivity and processes by that type of approach. If I see a big difference in

where we were three years ago and where we are now, it's much more about embedding technology into the business initiatives and the business strategies.

The earlier approach, in Archie's view, said, "Here's the Internet, let's bang it up and see what benefit we can get out of it." Or "Let's get a whole bunch of Internet-based accesses out there with all sorts of websites, and get all sorts of eyeballs on it and see how we can benefit from it." Today, he sees businesses moving away from that type of approach toward end-to-end business strategies, with technology intelligently applied to meet the needs of the business.

Another point of view, from Dave Clementz—

Most IT projects start off as an idea, and then the money gets spent, the software is bought, and people are starting to install it before they really think through, 'What the hell is this going to do for us in the end, and how am I going to integrate with everything else I've got.'

That phrase 'Go slow to go fast' means taking a lot of time up front in planning a project, wondering about all the possible things you need to worry about to get the project deployed. You begin with the end in mind, just like an engineering project; you see that structure you want to have at the end—[and you ask yourself] how do you do it, what does it take to get it there. We drive for a best-in-class, front-end loading index before we begin the project. We benchmark against ourselves and our prior projects.

When we've built all this and we understand all the variables to a high degree, then it's, 'Now let's go and do it and we'll learn as we go.' But people can't say we didn't put enough in the front end.

On the subject of checkpoints, especially as they were used on the massive IT effort involving the merger of Chevron with Texaco—

Other companies use checkpoints along the way in their engineering departments, for major projects like building a new plant; what we did is to adopt the engineering approach for the IT company. We call it a project development and execution process. It's the steps you take to do a project, all the way from conceiving the idea and trying to understand what the alternatives are, to planning, all the way to the operating and looking back on how it's running.

I had a group of people very, very early on in the merger do this big project. On this one, we modified our process to really beef up the reliability issue because we wanted to make sure that was well covered.

Do other companies use this engineering approach for IT projects? I don't know that anybody has it for IT, though of course they have checks and balances and milestones that you have to meet on these large projects. But it's just an adaptation, it's not rocket science.

At GMAC-RFC, Rick Greenwood's people do more than just lay a workflow out at the start of a project; they take the effort much further—

We go through and look at all the different connection points that we get information from. We look at the value of that information. How valid is it? Are there other ways that we could supply that information?

The other critical part is to build an automated workflow, and then to build rules that we show to the business for them to make their changes. So that another key part of that project going forward is that as we lay the process out, it does not have to be managed or constrained by having IT people making those changes.

We need the business people to understand the rules that they're putting in place, and decide what order they want them to be applied in, which one has preference over which other. So we spend an excruciating amount of time going through the rules and rule definitions—because once the business people understand that, they will later be able to go in and make the changes themselves. They'll know how to check to see if a new rule applies in a test environment, then add that to production without having to have IT involved.

Tips, Tricks and Tactics

A potpourri of ideas worth noting, beginning with more from Roger Smith on the 80/20 issue—

Our infrastructure management is to the point where we do view infrastructure much like turning on the tap for water. That part is commoditized, it's dependable, we know what to expect, we get what we expect, so we're happy.

The money might be 80-20 [infrastructure versus innovation], but the intellectual capital is probably 80-20 the other way. So we'll spend more thinking time on the question of 'Where should we be?' Put another way, a lot of that is focused on the customer—where it should be.

Roger has another rule of thumb, as well—this one for the planning phase of a proposed new technology project:

My assumption is based on the one-third test that's probably true in most businesses. We assume that one-third of our colleagues are going to actively embrace a new process or technology. And some portion—maybe up to another third—will have a take-or-leave-it attitude. The other third just don't get it, they'll use only part of it or they won't use it at all. It isn't that they don't embrace technology, it is more that for this group, the personal value proposition just isn't there. It's this gap that we need to explore. Regardless of the answers it delivers, it's the vetting process that's important. So in our focus groups, we use an approach of, 'Okay, who isn't going to like this? And should they? Within your group, where are the sticky points?'

It might break down by geography; we're always facing geographical issues since our Northeast Region has seven offices, many very large, and the South has seventeen offices, many quite small. So we look for geographical nuances, technology, people, process, whatever. We also look at reactions by discipline: 'Service will love this and our consultants can't wait, the head of sales has told us thanks but no thanks.' And then we have to make a decision how much drilling down, or mandating, we need to do.

We're pretty diligent on pilot testing, though we've had mixed success because our desire is to industrial-strength-test whatever process and technology we develop.

We have people who are eager beavers and spend a lot of time they don't tell us about to make things work. So we've had to be pretty harsh with the pilot groups, telling them to keep accurate track of their time. If we have some idea that this should take two minutes, when it takes twenty, we want to know what they were doing in that twenty minutes.

The biggest challenge is people just don't have the patience, they want the new solution now, while we're trying to be really diligent in each step to make sure when they get it, it works well. There is also a glass half empty/half full exercise I found helpful. An influential colleague voice may say, 'This solution only does half of what I need—but I understand, and the half it does is really great. I'll use what I can until the other functionalities come out.' Or a colleague may say—of the same application—'This solution only does half of what I need. I don't understand why, and I don't want to use it until the other half is addressed.'

You want to be ahead of this curve and know which side of this your major stakeholders are going to be on, then plan or adjust your approach accordingly.

The former CIO of JetBlue Airlines, Jeff Cohen, offered an intriguing suggestion for saving money from the IT budget—even though it's an approach that clearly wouldn't work if everybody tried it. He referred to it as "leveraging your technology partners."

If I do business with Microsoft or another major software supplier in such a way that I'm considered on the inside track, and I do all the things necessary to leverage technology, I gain a big advantage. We did that. I embraced technology to such a point that other companies came to me wanting to use JetBlue as a test platform for their new technologies.

That helps save money. The companies send lots of people who come on site and work with your teams. Your people get lots of training. All kinds of things basically come free.

Some companies will tell a supplier, 'We want to employ your technology, let me into your Beta program.' They get into the program, they're given fifty PCs, and they put them into a lab somewhere. At JetBlue, we actually put the Betas into production.

A lot of IT leaders wouldn't want to risk that, arguing that Beta software, by definition, can be expected to crash and be generally unreliable. Jeff doesn't see the issue that way—

Companies support their Beta technology very well. There really is no downside to putting in Beta software. I don't care what software you use, on any given day you're going to have some problems with it. When you have Beta technology, the developer responds instantaneously to your problems.

So, how do you do IT at an inexpensive price? One way you do it is by getting a reputation of being one of the most technologically advanced companies in America. That takes some work, it takes some time to get there. But once there, lots of companies come knocking on your door wanting a piece of the action—wanting to be able to say that they had your company as part of their launch platform. People are putting software on your machines for minimal cost, or for no cost.

There's a lot of money to be saved that way.

Picking up on a story introduced in an earlier chapter, one of our small-company entrepreneurs talks about an instance of a little guy passing along a technology idea to a giant. It happened when fiber-optics systems manufacturer Timbercon found they were in line to do a major project for a major aerospace company. Eric Meslow—

One of our key customers required us to centralize the information on our project for them. It turned out that they didn't know about the SharePoint server. And now this customer is excited about using it themselves.

This particular customer does chiefly military projects, they have a multitude of compliance personnel who make sure the project is going by the letter. By posting our updates and project information on a Microsoft SharePoint server, they're able to watch in real time as we update and make changes to the schedule.

By utilizing this type of centralized information, we've been able to reduce communication lag time, mass mailing and e-mailing to all parties involved, and project or schedule revisions. For the customer, this project is going to be real time and completely centralized. We'll also provide a customer log-in that allows them to make edits and changes on their end in real time.

When you're small like we are, and you're dealing with large customers and competing against large, very savvy competitors, one of the things that's always important is perception. A company like ours often lives or dies on it. The perception we have to project is that we've really got our stuff together—even if sometimes we're missing some resources that a larger competitor may have.

But for Timbercon, teaching a major client about a software-based work process capability wasn't just a matter of perception—

By setting up a large server with them, we can trade purchase orders, quotes, engineering drawings, project schedules, and everything like that. This may eliminate four or five site visits, and for us, that can add up to real money.

From south of the border, a story about technology leading to a wise use of funds at the Mexican oil production company Pemex, from a woman on the business side, Lic. Jazmín Loaiza. This is not so much a useful lesson (not many of us need to deal with decisions involving the location of gas wells) as it is a powerful little tale about learning to use technology effectively—

> If we don't have information, we don't know if the [exploration wells] are good or not. The system that had the technical information is not in a form for the decision makers. When a decision maker has to have information, he needs to ask someone to get it from the computer system for him. If the person he counts on for this gets sick, he cannot obtain the information.

The company launched a project to bring together all the information scattered in various places around Pemex—integrating it all in a simple way to make it accessible—

> Now we have the system that is so friendly that even the manager can consult information.
>
> At the beginning of the year I programmed ten wells. Now we have the information in the right time, we know if we are investing in a project with a good value or if we are losing money.
>
> If we know right now that a drilling project is not working, I can move the money to another project that maybe is giving better results than we expected. We are not talking about moving a team of one or two people; we are moving an exploration or gas production team. That implies a lot of people and a lot of expense. We are talking about millions and millions of dollars.

Sometimes we forget how much difference a simple, comprehensive database can make.

Short Takes on This and That

Some other miscellaneous ideas worth sharing. First, from the Army's Dave Borland—

> I think it's incredibly important to understand your long-term objective, and instead of putting together one massive program, you devise a bunch of individual programs that lead you in the

direction of that overall goal. You take an incremental approach to your long-range objectives.

Under our Army Knowledge Management Program, we have nine or ten initiatives that have to do with infrastructure, which we're doing as separate programs—in the area of directories, server consolidations, organizational consolidations, budget consolidations, and so on. So we have those all going down separate tracks parallel to each other, and they'll meet out there at some time in the future.

And from Marsh's Roger Smith, on avoiding unpleasant surprises—

What we try to do is eliminate the surprises and eliminate the obstacles that will kill the process early.

I'm sure everybody sees this all the time: 'Well, yeah, that will work in San Jose, but it won't work in Los Angeles because they have different area codes.' We try to eliminate the obvious obstacles as early as possible. And then we're open to changes along the way; we recognize that our colleagues, as they get their hands wet with the technology, will come up with additional features that they didn't think of at the beginning. So we're mindful of scope creep—the almost inevitable pressure toward gradual expansion in the scope of the project. But we're also open to the fact that there could be additional benefits.

We spend many hours on the transactional, mechanical part of what we do. It's about a three to one ratio over the strategic time. This is a challenge to us. There is a lot of work behind the scenes on transactional steps that put insurance products and solutions in place. However, our clients expect us to do this correctly without always providing them every process step in excruciating detail.

For example, explaining to the clients every step of an 84-step process is not really what they're are interested in. They're interested in consultative, strategic delivery of a business solution that enables them to meet a business need. Part of our technology paradox is that some of our technology must support the transactional as well as the consultative. Again, an on-going challenge of balancing infrastructure and cutting edge.

Dave Clementz, on saving money with technology—

There's still an appetite out there for the enlightened business unit that wants to save money by moving a physical process to something that's digital. You show me any operating expense sheet, any G&A structure, and I'll show you a place where you can save money using information systems.

There's no shortage of opportunities to add value. And most business units aren't out looking for those opportunities.

Washington Mutual's CIO has been weighing the question of going offshore—

A number of hot-button issues right now, I think, are tough to deal with. One is cross-border outsourcing. WaMu has actually been late coming to the table on this; we haven't done this kind of outsourcing yet. We're evaluating this right now. It's not black or white, there's some cherry picking that can be done here.

A lot of people are out of work, and Capitol Hill is now weighing in on this with concerns about all the jobs being shifted offshore. If I don't look at it, my successor will, because it is now more of an issue of remaining competitive.

You have to look at things that are important to you as an IT organization in maintaining your customer value proposition. United Airlines outsourced their dinner menus a long time ago, right? So there are some things in an IT shop that our customers don't care whether we do or not, and we could consider outsourcing those.

Right now we're looking at things like testing, which requires a lot of work; it's a big piece of any development project. No first-class software engineers like to do that stuff; they like to be cutting their code. So we're looking at those types of sweet spots, as I call them, where it could enable us to deliver products a lot more rapidly. We can get some cost efficiencies out of it and at the same time focus our people on designing and building solutions as opposed to maintaining and supporting legacy systems.

Somebody once said a paperless office is about as useless as a paperless bathroom. But paper isn't the point. The paper is where the forms sit that represent a process, and the process is what needs to be looked at. Ultimately you have to deal with that to eliminate the paper. Stan Hupfeld's view: "I think the reason we probably lose in our desire to go paperless is because somebody tells us we ought to. We probably lose the why of wanting to go paperless."

Technology, Tenacity, and Common Sense at Denver Health

As the final voice in this chapter, we want to introduce you to an unusual woman. Dr. Patty Gabow first showed up thirty years ago at Denver Health (back then called Denver General) as a young renal physician. In time she became Chief of Medicine, and for some years has been the CEO and Medical Director.

Denver Health is viewed as a national model for delivering health care in the public sector. The hospital is one of the busiest in the state of Colorado, and is a regional Level I Trauma Center. Their health clinics in the inner city handle some 400,000 outpatient visits a year. They have a very active Poison Center that answers local calls and calls from surrounding states. The list of major services and unusual contributions to the health care of their area goes on and on.

We wondered why a physician would give up the practice of medicine to become an administrator, and Dr. Gabow explained—

> Denver Health was having some major problems, and I really felt this was an institution that had enormous potential. When you're young, you believe you can do anything. I thought I could help even though I had no formal training in management.
>
> I actually think health care management is very much like taking care of a patient. When there's an issue, you need a diagnosis and you need a treatment plan, then you need to monitor your treatment plan and if it's not having the outcome you expected, you have to go back and either change the diagnosis or change your treatment. To me, that's what management is as well.
>
> I've seen a times when administrators don't actually make a diagnosis. They diagnose a symptom but they never get down to diagnosing the disease. It has served me well to think of taking care of the system as the same as taking care of people.

As an illustration of her point about diagnosing the disease, Dr. Gabow offered the following:

> Nine years ago, we used to drive the medical records around the city in the back of a truck—for half a million visits a year. You can imagine how often the patient, the doctor, and the

record ever got together at the same time. Today that whole system has been replaced by a single electronic record with a single patient identifier. It's all electronic; our clinics are paperless.

We've put over $100 million into information technologies since '96. This ready availability of information has contributed to making the quality of our care quite extraordinary, particularly when you realize we treat a very disenfranchised population. Forty percent of all our charges are to people who are uninsured.

Asked how she managed to make the dollar-equation work given that patient population, she flashed her sense of humor: "I print money in the basement." Her real answer—

I think our operational independence from any arm of government has been part of our secret.

Although Denver Health historically had been an institution of city government, Dr. Gabow a few years back managed to pull off an impressive coup: she convinced the powers-that-be to establish the public health care system as its own separate governmental entity. Today, the system has the best of both worlds: an independent, non-city governing board and a close relationship with city government. As Dr. Gabow told the Mayor when the new structure was created, "This is not a divorce, we just need to live in a different house."

Dr. Gabow has an additional explanation for the financial health of the organization—

Using information technology effectively is the other part. I always believed that we could find technological solutions to some of our dilemmas. A great example is our billings. About five or six years ago, we were doing about 10 percent of it electronically; now we do 75 percent electronically and get a clean bill out the door very quickly, which is important for us for cash flow.

With 27 percent of our patients non-English speakers, you can imagine the situation that a doctor faced—you've seen the patient, you don't have the chart, they can't speak English, and you can't speak their language. It's a patient safety issue, and a cost issue because the physician may very well be ordering tests or procedures that have just recently been done. That single electronic record has been an important part of the solution.

Looking back, Dr. Gabow described the unusual route the medical center followed once they had committed to the idea of innovating with technology—

> We decided that we weren't going to have the usual kind of customer/vendor relationship. We weren't going to go that way—we were going to have a partnership, a relationship. So we partnered with SMS, which has now become Siemens.
>
> That was extremely helpful because they worked jointly with us to understand our needs and develop solutions. We formed a very broad-based long-range systems planning committee; the group is so large that it fills our whole boardroom. We have representation from physicians, particularly physicians who are technologically savvy, and also physicians who had been the biggest critics of our old technology. We also have representation from nurses, ancillary services providers, and administrators. I think that decision proved to be a very good one.
>
> We also really made a point that whenever we moved to a new deployment of technology, we always made site visits to places where it was installed. We tried to learn what was working and what wasn't from the front line people.

Any number of comments appear in these pages cautioning against applying technology to an existing process that is flawed. Dr. Gabow offered her own experience on the subject—

> When we started looking at going to an electronic schedule, we said, 'We don't want to take technology and use it to sustain a dysfunctional process. Let's step back and redesign our appointment systems.' We want to be able to use technology to support the process we designed, rather than letting technology enable us to continue bad processes. That turns out to be a very hard thing to do.
>
> Then on July 1st [2003], we went paperless. We had had this wonderful electronic system up for a long time, but nobody wanted to give up the paper records. Because of the economy and a tremendous increase in our uninsured patient load, we were looking at a cash flow problem this year for the first time ever. In mid-May, I said, 'We have the technology, we're going to get rid of all this paper that we're pushing around, we're going paperless July 1st.' It wasn't much notice, but we did it. And actually it was pretty painless.

I haven't gotten one angry e-mail, which is one of my indicator of how well something works.

[As well,] when we went paperless in our clinics, we had thirty clerical positions that we were able to downsize or reassign to other needed duties.

It's kind of unusual to be able to point to a given intervention and demonstrate a cost savings. As an example, I believe having electronic medical records that avoid duplication of tests, procedures, and visits has saved us a great deal of money, but it's hard to demonstrate cost avoidance.

The transition from physician to business leader of a large organization is fairly unusual. Mrs. Gabow takes a long-term perspective—

My son once said to me, 'You never come home and say you've had a great day like you did when you took care of patients.' And I said, 'That's because when you run an institution, you don't have great days, you have great decades.'

It takes that long to transform them.

Take-Aways

Ideas seem limitless when you talk to the kinds of people who are included in this book. The issues raised in this final chapter represent subjects that stand out when people of insight think about technology, becoming a kind of checklist for items we all need to keep track of. In fact, as you'll notice, most of these apply not just when you're focusing on technology, but in a broader sense to many issues in business—

- Control the costs
- Mitigate the risks
- Engage the people
- Evaluate the payoff
- Learn from each other
- Pay attention to reliability and security
- Leverage your suppliers
- Never stop training and educating

And what better way to close this whole discussion than with the story we heard from Denver Health, where we were talking about an industry— healthcare—that is of such fundamental importance to everyone, yet that by the admission of its leaders is not fully leveraging the opportunity to take advantage of technology.

Healthcare stands as a reminder to all of us of how much we still have to learn about using technology to gain business value. The progress made at Denver Health also makes clear that leadership from the top is critical to realizing the full potential from our investments in information technology.

Profiles

Lawrence Baxter, Executive Vice President and Chief eCommerce Officer, Wachovia Corporation

A native of South Africa, Lawrence received his undergraduate degree in business, a law degree, and a Ph.D. in Law and Government Regulation, from the University of Natal. He continued his education in England, receiving a LL.M. and a Dip. in Law, both from the University of Cambridge. Lawrence is a member of the North Carolina Bar Association and Fourth Circuit Federal Court of Appeals, as well as the Supreme Court of South Africa. He is a member of the IT Advisory Board of Duke University Law School and the Board of the eBusiness Institute of the College of Technology at the University of North Carolina-Charlotte.

As leader of the Wachovia Bank's eCommerce Division, Lawrence works to protect the delicate balance between customers' privacy and using customer information to provide better products and services. He is responsible for developing, implementing and managing Wachovia's online strategy, marketing, and operations. Former duties have included director of Digital Financial Services; Emerging Businesses manager; special counsel for strategic development; and strategic consultant for the Financial Management and Legal Divisions.

Wachovia Corporation is a diversified financial services company that provides a broad range of banking, asset management, wealth management, and corporate and investment banking products and services. With more than 87,000 employees, the company is able to serve banking, brokerage, and corporate customers primarily on the East Coast, as well as through investment banking offices in selected locations. Global services are provided through thirty-two international offices.

The original Wachovia, founded in 1879 in Winston, North Carolina, and First Union, founded in 1908 in Charlotte, North Carolina, merged in September 2001 to create Wachovia Corporation.

David Borland, Deputy Chief Information Officer, U.S. Army

Dave Borland was born in Philadelphia, raised in New Jersey, and holds an undergraduate degree in Business Administration, and a Masters of Science Degree in Finance, from George Washington University in Washington, D.C. He began his work for the government as an intern for the Army Material Command, and spent most of his early career working in the field of information systems technology and contracting. Among his numerous government awards have been the Meritorious Presidential Rank Award and the Distinguished Presidential Rank Award. In 2000, *Government Computer News* magazine named him the Department of Defense Executive of the Year.

Lt. General Steven Boutelle, CIO, U.S. Army

Lieutenant General Boutelle started his military career in 1969, having enlisted in the Army as a Nuclear Weapons Electronics Specialist. Although he was born in Pasco, Washington, he claims Gig Harbor, Washington, as his home of record. He holds an MBA from Marymount University, Arlington, Virginia and has attended the Command and General Staff College, the Defense Systems Management College, and the Army War College.

A year after his Army enlistment, in February of 1970, Boutelle was commissioned as a second lieutenant in the Signal Corps at the Field Artillery Officer Candidate School, Fort Sill, Oklahoma. After service in Germany, he was given command of B Company, 58th Signal Battalion at Fort Lewis, Washington. Later he was assigned as Site Chief of the Main Command Post Korea, and subsequently as the Commander, 362nd Signal Company in Seoul, Korea.

The general holds military decorations including the Distinguished Service Medal, Legion of Merit with Oak Leaf Cluster, Defense Meritorious Service Medal, and the Army Meritorious Service Medal with four Oak Leaf Clusters.

Joe Capps, Director of Enterprise Systems Technology, U.S. Army

Joe Capps served in the Army from 1984 through 1988. He received his Bachelors degree in electrical engineering from Texas A&M University in 1991.

In 1992, Mr. Capps entered government civilian service, getting heavy-duty experience in research, development, and engineering. His assignments have included positions at the Army Research Laboratory, the Missile Command Research, Development and Engineering Center, and the Communications Electronics Command.

David M. Clementz, CIO, ChevronTexaco, and President and Chief Information Officer of the ChevronTexaco InformationTechnology Company

The story of Dave Clementz's unusual road to becoming chief of technology at a major global company without a technology background is told in Chapter 2.

A former Marine Corps officer, he holds an undergraduate degree from the University of Arizona, a master's degree from Purdue University, an MBA from Pepperdine University, and a Ph.D. from Michigan State University in soil science.

Now retired from ChevronTexaco, he is an executive vice president at EDS.

ChevronTexaco is the fourth largest publicly traded company worldwide in terms of oil and gas reserves, with some 11.9 billion barrels of reserves at the end of 2002. It also ranks as the fourth largest producer, with daily production of 2.6 million barrels of oil and gas. The company has twenty-three refineries and more than 24,000 retail outlets (including affiliates) worldwide.

Chevron Corp. merged with Texaco Inc. in 2001 to form the present company.

Jeff Cohen, former CIO, JetBlue Airlines

In one of the most unusual routes to the CIO's office, Jeff Cohen grew up in the New York area, and earned a degree in biology at the State University of New York, Stonybrook, with the intention of becoming a dentist. Instead, he ended up spending fifteen years in the clothing business, with technology as a hobby. Finally he started his own technology consulting company, at first working with homeowners, then with small companies, and moving on to mainstream corporations.

JetBlue Airways Corporation, based at John F. Kennedy airport, New York, is a low-fare, low-cost airline that started service in

February 2000. Three years later, the company was achieving annual revenues approaching the $1 billion level.

Susan Conway, Industry Director, Information Work Productivity Council

As Industry Director, Susan drives Microsoft's participation in the IWPC and guides the functioning of the Council. Previously she served as the manager of Worldwide Services Knowledge Management Communities of Practice, within Microsoft Consulting Services.

Susan completed her bachelors and master work at California State University, and earned her doctorate from Columbia Pacific University. She has spent a number of years developing and managing corporate skills, resource allocation, and technical project management programs in large enterprises such as Texaco Refining & Marketing, Computer Sciences Corp, and NCR. Susan is the author of *Unlocking Knowledge Assets* (Microsoft Press, 2002) and a contributing author to the *Handbook on Knowledge Management,* Springer-Verlag, 2002).

Craig Cuyar, CIO and Senior Vice President, CommonHealth

Craig Cuyar has full global responsibility for IT matters over all of the CommonHealth independent companies. He started on the provider side of the healthcare industry, gaining extensive knowledge in the use of large enterprise systems for clinical records, financial systems, physician billing systems in individual practices, and home healthcare. Prior to CommonHealth, he was the CIO of a healthcare system in Pennsylvania.

Born in Dallas, Craig grew up in Pittsburgh and currently resides in Randolph, New Jersey. Though he holds a Bachelors Degree, Masters Degree and Ph.D. from Penn State, he is, in addition to his more-than-full-time day job, currently working on an MBA at Rutgers.

CommonHealth, with headquarters in Parsippany, New Jersey, is the world's leading healthcare communications network, with sixteen operating units and an expertise in health-related brands in nearly every therapeutic category. CommonHealth provides advertising, marketing, promotion and medical education services to all of the world's largest pharmaceutical organizations and represents over 135 brands in the market today.

David Farquhar, Chief Operating Officer, Interactive University

In the late 1980's, after serving for eight years as an officer in the British Army, David moved into the commercial world as an entrepreneur specializing in the commercialization of mobile and wireless technologies. He subsequently built a series of companies in Scandinavia and the UK in markets including mobile enterprise applications. As an independent entrepreneur, he has co-founded or invested in several businesses in enterprise software, mobile technologies, drinks brand management, on-line recruitment, and a brew pub chain. He also co-created the original concepts for the Glasgow Science Centre and the GlobalScot Network.

Interactive University, based in Edinburgh, Scotland, was established in 2002, growing out of work by its founders over the course of several years in conjunction with Heriot-Watt University. The goal is to create a radical new model for global learning, with courses offered at many different levels, from foundation to doctorate.

Interactive University's Scholar program is the largest online learning solution in the world with over 45,000 students and almost four thousand tutors. The program offers more than ten thousand hours of online content specifically written for more than twenty different courses including Biology, Chemistry, Physics, Mathematics, French, English, and Computing, delivering 4.5 million on-line learning hours globally each year. All Scholar courses allow students to share their knowledge in real-time online communities.

The IU courses are created by a Scottish university or college to guarantee high academic standards.

Dr. Patricia Gabow

Dr. Patricia Gabow was originally recruited to Denver Health from San Francisco General to start a renal (kidney) service that was desperately needed in the Denver community. Over the thirty years since then, she has changed the model under which Denver Health functions to promote continuity of care and avoid inefficiencies. Under her leadership, by fully integrating public hospitals and community health centers, Denver Health now serves as a model for health care in the U.S. (For fascinating details of her achievements in leading the institution to this position, see Chapter 10.)

Denver Health is a remarkable umbrella institution providing medical care in a broad range of areas: Colorado's largest health-care provider; a Poison and Drug Center serving Colorado and some of the surrounding states; a Level 1 Trauma Center; paramedic services; and community health clinics throughout the area, among other activities.

As Colorado's primary "safety net" institution caring for vulnerable members of the community, Denver Health has in the last ten years provided more than $1.4 billion worth of care for the uninsured. One in every four Denver residents receives their health care at Denver Health. One of every three children in Denver is cared for by Denver Health physicians.

Richard Greenwood, CIO, Residential Capital Group, GMAC-RFC

After graduating from a small college in Minnesota, Rick Greenwood accepted a position with an accounting/financial firm, followed by work as a consultant and positions at Control Data and then at Hewlett Packard, where he became well versed in RISC architecture. From Hewlett Packard, Rick accepted a management position within 3M, initially with responsibilities for distributed technologies, later becoming responsible for all of the manufacturing applications.

Rick originally joined GMAC-RFC as Chief Technology Officer, responsible for architecture, infrastructure and production operations.. He became CIO of the company's Residential Capital Group in October 2000.

GMAC-RFC's Residential Capital Group offers mortgage products and technology solutions to residential mortgage lenders and mortgage brokers. The group is the nation's leading private issuer of mortgage-backed and mortgage related asset-backed securities.

Jeremy V. Gross, Executive Vice President and Chief Information Officer, Washington Mutual, Inc.

Born in Melbourne, Australia, Jerry's education started at a kindergarten called "Little St. Margaret's." After earning a business degree at Monash University in Melbourne, Jerry's career began at a local firm where he did basic accounting. A position with KPMG

Consulting brought him to Los Angeles in the 1980's, and he subsequently held a position at Countrywide Credit Industries, where he became managing director and chief technology officer. In that role, he led the company's technology innovation that resulted in the origination of the first online mortgage loan in the U.S.

Jerry also built the first business-to-business extranet in the nation. He later worked at the Australian bank Westpac, where he was the executive in charge of technology, operations, and e-commerce.

In 2001, Jerry accepted his current position at Washington Mutual.

Washington Mutual, Inc. (WaMu) is a national retailer of financial services with a history dating back to 1889.

In 1962, when WaMu installed its first computer (an IBM 1401 the size of a refrigerator, with 4k of memory), a local newspaper wrote that it was "the first savings bank west of Minneapolis to install so advanced a computer system."

Washington Mutual was also the first bank to acquire a full-service securities brokerage firm. Today WaMu is widely recognized as one of the nation's leading and fastest-growing financial services companies.

Steve Hankins, CFO, Tyson Foods

Steve Hankins earned his MBA at the age of 21 but still looked like a high schooler. His youthful appearance, despite his degrees, couldn't get him the believability he needed to fulfill his goal of becoming a consultant.

A pragmatic decision prompted Steve to take a job with a small poultry company, Hudson Foods, in a plant located near his home in northwest Arkansas. After a few years he moved on to Tyson Foods, where he rapidly advanced from simple cost accounting and finance. He became responsible for all the company's operational accounting in the late 1980's. In 1990 he took over the leadership of the Information Systems area, growing from 19 professionals to over 250 in a seven-year period, while the company grew from just under $2 billion in sales to over $7 billion. He became CFO in 1998.

Tyson Foods, Inc., founded in 1935 with headquarters in Springdale, Arkansas, is the world's largest processor and marketer of chicken, beef and pork. With annual revenues of $24 billion, Tyson is the second largest food company in the Fortune 500. The company has approximately 120,000 employees, with offices in 27 states and 22 countries.

Stan Hupfeld, CEO, Integris Health

Stan Hupfeld grew up in Texas, attended the University of Texas, and played on the 1963 Texas national champion university football team. Service in Vietnam as a Battalion Surgeon's Assistant stirred an interest in health care. After earning a graduate degree, Stan worked in this field in El Paso and Fort Worth, Texas, before being offered the position of President of Baptist Medical Center, in Oklahoma City.

Under Hupfield's seventeen-year leadership, the hospital had grown in both scope and facilities; in the mid-90's, he led a merge of the Center with two other entities to form Integris Health.

Integris Health, Inc., is a not-for-profit corporation formed to serve as the parent corporation for Baptist Medical Center and related entities. The predecessor institution that opened in 1959 was first known as the "hospital on the hill"; at the time, it was reached by a dirt road, and surrounded by just a few homes. But the hospital quickly grew and its impact was felt throughout Oklahoma; it's now the largest provider of hospital services in the state, with hospitals, rehabilitation centers, physician clinics, mental health facilities, independent living centers, and home health agencies. Outlying facilities and services serve much of the state of Oklahoma.

S. Kregg Jodie, Executive Vice President & Chief Information Officer, Mary Kay Inc.

Kregg Jodie holds a bachelor of business administration degree in electrical engineering from the University of Texas at Austin.

Prior to Mary Kay Inc., Kregg was employed by Accenture, providing management expertise for organizations such as Hertz Corporation, Federal Express, and the Federal Aviation Administration.

He joined Mary Kay in 1993 as manager of sales force automation, and became CIO in 1997.

Mary Kay Inc. is one of the largest direct sellers of skin care and color cosmetics in the world, with more than 1.1 million independent sales force members worldwide, some 650,000 in the U.S. alone. Sales in 2002 topped $1.6 billion, and the company has averaged double-digit annual growth throughout its 40-year history.

Since inception, the company has followed the philosophy of founder Mary Kay: God first, family second, and career third.

Archie Kane, Group Executive Director, Lloyds TSB plc (Lloyds Bank, Great Britain), and Chief Executive, Scottish Widows

Archie Kane is one of those people who has had a career on both the business and the technology sides of the house. He is a Chartered Accountant (the British equivalent of a CPA), and holds an undergraduate degree from Glasgow University and an MBA from City University Business School, London. He has also completed the Advanced Management Program at Harvard Business School.

He currently holds a position on the board of directors of Lloyds, as Group Executive Director for Insurance and Investments. In 2003, he also became the Chief Executive of a subsidiary, the Group's long-term insurance company, Scottish Widows.

Before joining Lloyds in 1994, Archie served as Finance Director for a subsidiary of GTE in the UK. At Lloyds TSB he has held a variety of positions of increasing responsibility, among them Director of Financial Control for the Retail Banking Division, and then, crossing to the technology side, as Director of Group IT and Operations. He has served as a Group Strategic Development Director, responsible for strategic planning for all mergers and acquisitions for the banking group.

Outside the bank, Archie has served as Chairman of the APACS Council, the senior decision-making body of the UK payments industry, with responsibility for a wide range of matters involving cooperation in the development and delivery of payment and money transmission services.

Lloyds TSB plc is one of the leading financial services groups based in the United Kingdom, providing a comprehensive range of banking and finance in the U.K. and overseas. At the end of 2002, Lloyds had market capitalization of just under $U.S. 50 billion, with a staff of over 79,000 employees.

The main businesses are retail banking and mortgages, serving some 15 million customers; insurance and investments; wholesale markets, which manages relationships with major UK and multi-national companies and financial institutions; and international banking, serving Europe, the Americas, the Middle East and Asia.

Professor Roy Leitch, Chief Executive, Interactive University

Roy Leitch trained as an Electrical Engineer, graduating with BSc and PhD degrees from Heriot-Watt University, Edinburgh, and worked in the Petrochemical industries. During his academic career, he established and directed the 'Intelligent Systems Laboratory' at Heriot-Watt, working in the fields of process control and diagnostics, and industrial training systems.

As Deputy Principal at Heriot-Watt University, he has been responsible for developing and implementing the distinctive learning and teaching strategy that has placed that university at the forefront of educational innovation. The success of these initiatives has led to the establishment of the Interactive University, of which he is the founding Chief Executive Officer.

Roy is a Fellow of both the Institution of Electrical Engineers and the British Computer Society. He has consulted for the UK Government and Research Councils, EU research programs, and the Indian and Italian governments.

(For a thumbnail on Interactive University, see the David Farquhar profile, above.)

Lic. Jazmín Loaiza

Ms. Loaiza holds a Bachelor's Degree from Latinoamerican University of Communication and Public Relations, and a Master's Degree from La Salle University, México, in administration, with a specialty in enterprise finances. She has been with Pemex since 1993.

Pemex, Mexico's state-owned energy company, is the largest company in Mexico and the world's third largest petroleum companies in terms of crude oil output. The firm accounts for 10 percent of Mexico's exports and 37 percent of the government revenues.

As of January 2004, the company has some 4,100 producing wells, 185 offshore platforms, and six refineries.

Eric Meslow, Founder and President, Timbercon, Inc.

Eric Meslow was a high school graduate before computers took a firm hold in every classroom. He remembers being convinced by the time he graduated from college that everything his generation would ever do would be PC-driven.

Meslow, together with business partner James Davies, started Timbercon after working together at a Portland-area high-tech firm, where they were frustrated with the company's non-responsiveness to customers. Taking advantage of the boom climate of 1997, the two started the company in an extra bedroom of Eric's house. Within seven months, business had grown enough for the two to move into proper offices.

Timbercon, Inc., is a fiber optic product assembly and manufacturing company providing products for the telecommunications, data storage, and military vertical markets. The company has pioneered multiple new proprietary products, many of which are now considered to be industry benchmark items, such as their flagship Armadillo connector.

Timbercon is ranked as one of the fastest growing private firms in Oregon. Annual revenues are stated as approaching $5 million.

Rachelle Mileur, Director of eCommerce Systems Development, Airborne Express

Rachelle attended the University of Illinois, where she earned a Bachelor of Science in Computer Science and Accounting, graduating with highest honors.

During her professional career, Ms. Mileur has held positions with Andersen Consulting; with IBM Global Services as senior program manager and regional consulting manager; and as an independent consultant. Her special areas of expertise are managing systems integration projects, directing project offices, establishing offshore development processes, and leading development groups in support of transportation, financial, and retail businesses.

Airborne Express has been described as one of the fastest-growing air express delivery companies, serving every ZIP code in the U.S. and over 200 countries worldwide. Customers include more than 60 percent of the Fortune 500 companies. During peak season, Airborne's website tracking supports 1.3 million customer requests a day.

In 2003, Airborne completed its merger with DHL Worldwide Express.

Gary Moore, Senior Vice President, Cisco Systems, Inc.

As a student in industrial engineering, Gary Moore eventually figured out why he couldn't seem to learn to read the color coding of electrical resistors: he's color blind. His professor must have been pleased to see him graduate and leave campus, since he had blown up at least one elevator controller during his lab courses.

On leaving college, Gary joined the Army to do data processing and high-speed network communications, and on completing his tour joined EDS. There he became part of a leading-edge technology team and in time rose to the rank of senior vice president, heading one of four worldwide operations; he was responsible for e-Solutions and was leading 20,000 people.

Gary was selected at age 38 to become President and CEO of Hitachi Data Systems, at the time a subsidiary of Hitachi, Ltd., in Japan, with EDS as a minority owner. As planned, after three years in that position he returned to EDS, becoming President of EDS Japan. Gary subsequently became CEO of a Silicon Valley start-up. In 1999, he joined Cisco to run a new venture, the Advanced Services organization.

Cisco Systems, Inc. is considered the world's leading supplier of networking equipment and network management for the Internet. It provides a broad line of products for transporting data, voice, and video within buildings, across campuses and around the world. The company's products are installed at corporations, public institutions and telecommunication companies, as well as commercial businesses, and are also found in personal residences.

Headquartered in San Jose, California, Cisco has annual revenues of close to $20 billion. Cisco's number one priority and focus has always been on the success of their customers. The company mission is to stay committed to helping customers with securing their network environment through best practice sharing, and through innovative and resilient network products, technologies, and services.

John Rootenberg, MD

John D. Rootenberg is the Director of Information Technology and Services for Clinical Research at the University of California, San Francisco, as well as the Director of Informatics for the UCSF Department of Neurology. In addition to his background in clinical research and medicine, Dr. Rootenberg has more than fifteen years experience in information services business and strategic management consulting. His clients have included pharmaceutical and life sciences companies, advertising and marketing agencies, state and federal government agencies, and information technology companies. In addition, Dr. Rootenberg has served as a special advisor to the White House and U.S. Congress, a Senior Section Editor for the *Journal of the American Medical Association (JAMA),* and as a healthcare futurist for Accenture. He was previously the Executive Director of the Institute for Medical Information and Technology.

Prof. Lee Schlenker, École de Management (The Graduate School of Management), Lyon, France

Lee Schlenker serves as a full professor at the management school (École de Management) of the University of Lyon, and is also a visiting professor at the University of Newcastle, Newcastle on Tyne, England. A former senior mission director, he has been working over the last few years with major computer firms on collaborative technologies, virtual communities, and process-centric systems. Professor Schlenker holds a doctorate in political economy.

Karen Settle, CEO, Keystone Marketing Specialists, Inc.

Karen Settle has worked in retail, manufacturing, field marketing service, and training in high-tech industries for more than twenty-five years. Early on, she gained much of her training from industry giants Compaq Computer Corp. and the Xerox Corporation. Her expertise lies with the in-store experience, as well as in the training of resellers and retail-store associates.

Karen has been featured in *Entrepreneur, Inc,* the *Los Angeles Times,* and *Executive Female,* as well as appearing on CNBC's "Minding Your Business" and "How To Succeed in Business," and CNN/FN's "Business Unusual."

Keystone Marketing Specialists, based in Las Vegas, has since the early 1990's provided a North American field sales/support force in support of companies such as Logitech, AMD, IBM, Microsoft, and Symantec. Keystone field reps focus on in-store training of retail sales associates in major computer and technology stores across the

United States and Canada. The company's field reps and client managers work to help their high tech-clients gain market share, floor space, and increased sales.

Keystone fields a force of some 200 representatives and pulls in annual revenues of more than $5 million.

Roger H. Smith, Senior Vice President, Marsh Inc.

After earning a Bachelor of Arts degree from California Lutheran University, Roger Smith went to work as an underwriter with Chubb in New York City. He subsequently joined Frank B. Hall insurance brokers and worked in their Los Angeles and Honolulu offices. Along the way he qualified for the titles of Chartered Property and Casualty Underwriter, and Associate in Risk Management.

Roger joined Marsh in 1984 and has served the firm as a Head of Office and Practice Leader. He has also served as a member of the firm's technology governance and technology advisory committees.

His current responsibilities at Marsh include the position of Chief Quality Officer for the Western Region. In that position, he leads quality and process improvement initiatives under the banner of Marsh Excellence. He speaks frequently on focused customer solutions and customer relationships.

Marsh Inc., established in 1871, is the world's number one risk and insurance services firm. Marsh has 410 owned-and-operated offices in more than 100 countries, with 38,000 "colleagues," and generates annual revenues of approximately $6 billion.

The company is an operating unit of Marsh & McLennan Companies, Inc., a global professional-services firm with approximately 60,000 employees and annual revenues exceeding $10 billion.

Terry Szpak, Founder, Telesystems West

Terry was born in Ontario, Canada, grew up in Vancouver, and came to the U.S. after marrying a Minnesota girl. Like Bill Gates, he dropped out of college (Simon Fraser University and the British Columbia Institute of Technology) to go into the telecom industry. He worked for British Columbia Telecom and GTE, installing and maintaining telephone systems, before starting his company.

Telesystems West, based in Bellevue, Washington, has been selling and installing phone system solutions in the greater Puget

Sound area since 1963. The company has served over 5,000 customers. Telesystems primarily represents three major system vendors: Panasonic, Nortel, and Shoreline. Sales are $1.5 million to $2.0 million annually.

Carla A. von Bernewitz. Director, Enterprise Integration Oversight Office, U.S. Army

Reporting to the Under Secretary of the Army and Acting Secretary of the Army, Carla von Bernewitz has responsibility for guiding the development and transformation of Army business systems, with particular focus on Enterprise Resource Planning (ERP). Prior to assuming this position, Ms. von Bernewitz operated a private consulting practice advising client companies in planning for growth, innovation, and change. She specialized in policy formulation, strategic planning, cost/benefit trade-off studies, functional economic analyses, and information management, with domain expertise in logistics, the Federal government, supply chain management, and information architectures.

She holds a BS in Decision Science from George Mason University, and an MBA in Information Systems Management from George Washington University in Washington, D.C.

Prior to starting her consulting practice, Ms. von Bernewitz worked for Electronic Data Systems as Northeast Region General Manager. She was a Program Scientist with Vector Research, Incorporated where she conducted functional economic analyses and architecture studies for the Department of Defense.

She has also served on staff with the Defense Logistics Agency, where she was the Chief Information Officer and Executive Director of Information Systems and Technology. She worked as well for the Assistant Secretary of Defense, coordinating Year 2000 activities for sixty agencies.

David Wilson, President, East Industries

After college, Dave Wilson went to work for a fast track textile company that moved their top talent from plant to plant to invigorate startup operations. Over time he noticed something curious about wooden shipping pallets used by the local laboratory of a major pharmaceutical company: when pallets became damaged, they were tossing them into a pile in a remote corner of their property. The pallets are expensive, and Dave saw an opportunity.

He and a neighbor who became his partner initially offered companies the service of just getting rid of the damaged pallets for them. Once established in the removal business, they recognize the logical next step: repairing the damage and selling the restored pallets back to their customers.

That was twenty years ago. Since then, East Industries has become what Dave refers to as "a small business in a fast-growing, competitive industry." The success of that one company has permitted him to move simultaneously into running several others, as well.

East Industries, Inc, located in Rocky Mount, North Carolina, is a service company that today offers warehousing and storage, and pallet and packaging logistical support, as well as continuing in the original business of manufacturing and remanufacturing shipping pallets. The company reports annual revenues of $3 million.

From billing to the storage of trailer rentals, East Industries is considered expert at a myriad of value-added services to manufacturing companies. They have recently added a private information portal for customers, offered via the Web.

East Industries was chosen in 2003 to be showcased by Microsoft for its successful uses of technology.

Acknowledgments

Bob McDowell

This book would never have seen the printed page without the enthusiasm, encouragement, and efforts of many people at Microsoft. At the front of that parade is Jeff Raikes, an enthusiastic, charismatic leader in so many ways at the company. Jeff gets full credit for making this book possible; he understood from the first the importance of presenting a book with this dynamic message.

As with any project of this sort, there are so many people who have been of enormous help to Bill and me in the research and writing. But I do not hesitate for a moment in knowing where to begin. Lissa, my wife of 35 years, keeps me grounded yet inspires my mind to fly. I have never lost sight of her value and joy in my life. I am always grateful for Lissa's intelligence and unending support, which combine with her super-human patience over my yet-untamed energies.

The list of Microsoft people who have so willingly helped begins with Arthur Yasinski and Jeremy Nelson in Redmond. Teri Jensen and Kathleen Vilchez, my two remarkable assistants, merit high admiration of their organizational skills. In addition, Jacqueline Borges and Kathleen get a special nod of approval for help in suggesting a title for this book.

So many Microsoft field people helped us to synchronize the interviews and coordinate schedules with the people whose words and ideas fill these pages. Hopefully these words of appreciation will express our thanks to Catherine Boeger; Jack Elmore; Nancy Stickney; Debbie Daton; Carol Kerins ; Lisa Tanner, Mark Klein, & Scott Sealock; Ryan Mckinney, Rob Bradford, & Ashly Jungers; Debbie McMillen, Ryan McKinney, & Regina Rafraf Kienzle; Megan Holt; Carlos Serafin Rodriguez & Jose Olivera Beltran.

It's trite but absolutely true to say that this book would not have been possible without the cooperation of the more than thirty people who took their time to allow us to interview them, and to review their interview materials. So my special gratitude, and Bill's, goes to:

Lawrence Baxter, Diana Beecher, Dave Borland, Lt. General Steven Boutelle, Joe Capps, Dave Clementz, Avery Cloud, Susan Conway, Jeff Cohen, Craig Cuyar, Joe Eschback, David Farquhar, Dr.

Patricia Gabow, Richard Greenwood, Jerry V. Gross, Steven Hankins, Stan Hupfeld, Kregg Jodie, Archie Kane, Prof. Roy Leitch, Lic. Jazmín Loaiza, Eric Meslow, Rachelle Mileur, Gary Moore, John Rootenberg, MD, Prof. Lee Schlenker, Karen Settle, Roger Smith, Terry Szpak, Carla von Bernewitz, and David Wilson.

Finally, my primary pleasure in writing this book has been working again with Bill Simon. Though we became friends while writing *Driving Digital,* there's nothing like writing a book to put two people on the same wavelength. My admiration for Bill's talent, precision, and patience is only exceeded by my appreciation for his loyal friendship.

Bill Simon

Great thanks and appreciation go to my wonderful wife, Arynne, without whose comments, constant support, and encouragement my books would not have been written. It was she who seduced me into the writing of books and assured me that I could be as successful in print as I had been for so many years in the world of film and television.

From the time I first heard about this project, I knew that writing again with Bob McDowell would be a repetition of the pleasure I had enjoyed the last time around. Widely admired because he is so affable, pleasant, and a compelling public speaker, Bob is a wealth of information and ideas about the corporate use of technology as a result of his frequent meetings with CEOs, Chief Information Officers, and board members, around the world. More than that, Bob and his charming wife Lissa are wonderful hosts and good friends.

It is traditional and typical for the next words of appreciation to be directed at my friends and family but my tireless and loyal agent, Bill Gladstone, CEO of Waterside Communications, deserves to be acknowledged and appreciated. This is the 12th book that Bill has handled for me. Under his positive leadership, the people in his office—in particular David Fugate, Kimberly Valentini, and Maureen Malone—find ways to make my life as a writer easier; Gladstone and his team are a joy to work with.

And that is also also how I would describe Kenzi Sugihara, the principal of Select Books and the publisher of this book; he is a brilliant man and a joy to work with—a rare combination. A tip of the hat as well to editor Todd D. Barmann, whose keen eye, experience, alertness, and intelligence combined into the ability to point out a number of ways for strengthening the book.

Of the people at Microsoft who helped with research and coordination, I especially want to acknowledge Jeremy Nelson, who was tireless in his efforts and tremendously effective; if I were in charge, I'd be giving him a raise. In Bob McDowell's office, Teri saw only the beginning of the project but was ably replaced by Kathleen Vilchez, who helped out with an enthusiasm and eagerness that was always a pleasure. Field rep Catherine Boeger came through with excellent suggestions that made a significant difference. And to Ann Hamilton of Microsoft Press—my gratitude once again.

How often I impose my thoughts on my children Victoria Simon and Sheldon Bermont; their patient listening helps me keep my perspective through the months of writing each book. My family are all an intrinsic part of my writing team and I hope they will be patient as I tackle the many upcoming projects that Gladstone has lined up for me.

And my appreciation also goes to the many writers and thinkers whose works I read with awe, particularly Dickens, Le Carré, and Shakespeare.

Finally I again pay respects to the memory of my parents, but most especially my Dad, who painstakingly corrected my grammar (even including letters home from summer camp), and to television writer Sy Salkowitz, who breathed life into my career as a film writer. Both live in my memory and continue to inspire.

Appendix

Excerpts from the Technology Governance Template Used at Marsh

Marsh's Roger Smith, who provided this material, explains that the technology business case template was created "in order to obtain credible project proposals and/or business cases for all planned and existing applications. The template was for business leaders to use as their outline in preparing requests for technology projects."

As noted in Chapter 2, the questions intentionally focus more on people and processes issues than on technology.

The major categories of the template include—

Project Leadership
Project Description
Business/Strategic Impact
Colleague Impact
Process Impact
Technology Impact
Financial Impact
Performance Goals and Annual Review
Executive Summary

Some of the major questions in the template are as follows; (the parenthetical items are explanatory comments provided for our readers by Roger Smith).

Business/Strategic Impact

Give a brief background of the major aspects and trends of your business, such as historical and projected growth in market segments, market conditions and any other key factors. Copy any appropriate sections of your business plan. *(This is intended as a "heads-up" to the business. Yes, we will tie this proposed solution back to your business plan when measuring performance.)*

How will this project help you meet your business objectives in the long and short terms? *(This helps us frame the ROI.)*

What are the consequences if this project is not undertaken or is delayed? *(Business leaders often claim "We have to do this," so we decided to ask "What happens if we don't?" to gain insights.)*

Colleague Impact

Describe how users (colleague, client, underwriter, etc.) will be impacted by the application. *(We provide a chart asking for how many in each category.)*

a. **Discuss their readiness level, expected learning curve, overlap with related or predecessor applications and migration plan, time to load application with content and similar issues.**

b. **How will user acceptance be measured and validated? Will this solution be mandated?** *(Drilling down in the answers to this question provides very interesting subtext. If the solution is so good, why would it not be mandated? Is there a culture shift that must take place as well? Hint to the business—we do not accept "Build it and they will come" as an answer.)*

c. **Describe user role in design, testing, training, implementation, and on-going feedback.** *(Our view is the business has a place in each phase—any gaps we perceive here are explored and fixed.)*

d. **Describe and attach any relevant implementation, marketing, or communication plans.** *(The "stuff" we see here shows the extent to which an evolution is already being talked about, indicating to us a better chance for the technology solution to succeed.)*

Process Impact

How will this application improve current business processes? Explain how it could reduce cycle time, increase quality, or reduce errors. Attach diagrams of current and improved processes.

Identify the major components of your project. Assess their priority, explain dependencies, and discuss possible phasing of development and implementation. *(We know from experience that projects sometimes are delayed due to unforeseen circumstances—the answer to the question will enable us to prioritize later in the project.)*

Does your project interact with other systems? Explain dependencies not addressed above. *(Although we will provide corporate guidance here because we do not expect our business leaders to know every solution Marsh has, if they have some compare and contrast experience, we'd like to capture it here.)*

Glossary

For readers not familiar with common business abbreviations used in the United States, these few used in the book have the meanings shown—

B-school
A business school; in particular, a school that awards a graduate degree in business. The usage "the B-school" specifically refers to the Harvard Business School.

CEO
Chief Executive Officer—in the U.S. the title usually held by the most senior executive of the company, hired by and reporting to the company's board of directors. Frequently also carries the title of President.

CFO
Chief Financial Officer

CIO
Chief Information Officer—generally the person in charge of an organization's Information Technology department or group.

IT
An organization's Information Technology department or group.

ROI
Return on Investment—a measure of benefits (usually financial) derived from a particular project, product, or methodology. In one definition, the return (earnings) as a percentage of the assets employed (investment).

Index

A

Accountability, 84, 100
After-the-fact analysis, 81
After-the-fact audit process, 84
Airborne Express, 23–26
    Call Centers, 24
    eCommerce Systems
      Development, 23, 201
    innovations, 25–26
    operation, commodity perspective, 154–155
    Phoenix project, 45
    projects, delivery, 99
    technology cost, justification, 73–74
Audit process. *See* After-the-fact
    audit process
    direction, 84–88
    usage, 89–91
    validation, user surveys (usage), 93–94
AutoCAD, usage, 76

B

Back-office processes, 45
Ballmer, Steve, 103
Baxter, Lawrence, 49–50
    business requirements, 114
    change, need, 122
    discipline, 130
    governance, description, 99–100
    pressure, 167–168
    profiles, 191
    ROI, opinion, 71–72
    technology usage, 115–116, 162
Beta software, reliability, 181–182

Borland, David, 117, 124–125, 183–184
    profile, 192
Boutelle, Steven, 11–12, 121
    profile, 192
    ROI, opinion, 71
    technology change, 116–117
Business
    change, technology (impact), 115–119
    issues, technology (impact), 13–15
    managment, priorities, 86
    processes
      technology application, 72–73
      technology support, 43
    school (B-school), 213
    technology usage, 174–176
    value
      achievement, 3
      measurement, 65–67

C

Capps, Joe, 46–47
    profile, 192–193
Capture-and-combine approach, 175–176
Carr, Nicholas, 153–154, 156
    article/thesis, disputation, 155–163
Change. *See* Culture; Technology
    difficulty, 119–123
    management, 119
    reactions, 154–157
Chevron, merger, 51, 103–105, 131, 137, 178

ChevronTexaco, 21, 193
  CIO Council, 87, 104
  corporate IT team, 103
  Decision Review Board, 87
  Embedded IT Groups, 139–140
  Enterprise Group, 140
  Information Technology
    Company, 139–140
  internal customers, value
    (receiving), 137–138
  IT, 51
  management, 36
  Merger Integration Team, 51
  productivity benefit, 39
  project interference, 86–87
  reliability/security, 173
  standardization, 142–143
  technology usage, 120
  vision, 40
Chief Executive Officer (CEO), 20,
  213
Chief Financial Officer (CFO), 213
Chief Information Officer (CIO),
  13, 20, 213
  Chief Financial Officer (CFO),
    teamwork, 7–8
  role, rethinking, 138–141
Chief Technology Officer (CTO),
  16, 38
Christensen, Clayton, 168
Cisco Systems, Inc., 52–54, 202
  costs, reduction, 54
  e-learning capability, 52–53
  Internet Capabilities Team, 102
Clementz, David M., 21, 36–40
  business perspective, 139–140
  Carr article, opinion, 156–157,
    159, 160
  CIO Council, 51
  costs/money, recovery/saving,
    137–138, 184–185
  IT organization, change, 131
  IT oversight group, 103–105
  IT projects, initiation, 178

  look-back, 86–87
  outsourcing, opinion, 145
  profile, 193
  standardization, 142–143
  surprises, 51–52
  technology
    budget cuts, 123
    fascination, 120
  vision, 40
C-level officers, 14
Cloud, Avery, 33–36
COBOL, usage, 64–65
Cohen, Jeff, 142, 181
  profile, 193–194
Commodity input/technology,
  153–154
CommonHealth, 29–30, 194
  after-the-fact analysis, impact,
    81–83
  after-the-fact evaluations, 83–84
  auditing, impact, 85
  courier services, out-of-pocket
    costs, 30
  IT restructuring, 130–131
  merger/acquisition process, 124
  utility function, outsourcing,
    144
Companies (successful programs),
  governance lessons, 101–110
Competition, surpassing, 27–28
Competitive advantage, 158–159,
  177
  meaning, 29
  technology, usage, 22–29
Conway, Susan, 68–70
  profile, 194
Corporate leadership, assistance,
  105
Corporate merger, IT transition,
  51–52
Corporate technology, survival,
  176–177
Cost reduction, technology
  (usage), 29–33

Culture
  change, 76, 117, 123–126,
    132–133
  improvement, 113
Customers, technology usage,
  161–162
Cuyar, Craig, 8, 29–30
  after-the-fact analysis, opinion,
    81–83
  auditing, emphasis, 85
  business units, paradoxical rela-
    tionship, 138
  Carr article, opinion, 155–156
  consistency, achievement, 124
  IT problems, solutions, 130–131
  outsourcing, opinion, 144
  profile, 194
  value, burden, 83–84

D
Defensive Thinking.com, 173–174
Denver Health, 196
  example, 186–189
DHL, acquisition, 23, 45, 201
Downes, Larry, 117

E
East Industries, 18–20, 27–28,
  205–206
  accounting program, control,
    48–49
  pallet inventory management
    system, 32
  per-piece arrangement, 30–31
  technology usage, 30–32, 47–49,
    145–147
École de Management, 67, 203
  technology investment, 118–119
EDI technology, usage, 134–135
E-learning, 53
Employees, technology usage/ben-
  efit, 160–161
Empowerment, 91
End-to-end business strategies, 178
Enterprise solutions, 47

ERP software, 118
Eschbach, Joe, 129
Executives, technology usage, 6–7
External auditing, value, 79

F
FAA requirements, 23
Failure, demonstration, 84
Farquhar, David, 169, 170
  profile, 195
Federal Express, 30
  Airborne, competitive advan-
    tage, 24
Finance managers, rigor, 72
Financial model, 33
Food and Drug Administration,
  requirements, 30

G
Gabow, Patricia, 186–189
  profile, 195–196
General Motors Acceptance
  Corporation (GMAC), 6–7, 14,
  49, 130, 172
  auditing, priority, 83
  workflow, 179
Genomics information, usage,
  174–176
Governance
  change, 100–101
  usage, 97–100
Governmental agencies, competitive advantage, 29
Greenwood, Richard, 6–7, 14–15,
  49
  auditing, opinion, 83
  Carr article, opinion, 159
  change management, involve-
    ment, 119
  profile, 196
  project initiation, 179
  technology usage, 172–173
Gross, Jeremy V., 3–5, 12, 16,
  62–63
  auditing process, 93–94

Carr article, opinion, 158, 163–164
economic climate, IT (adapting), 176–177
governance, opinion, 101–102
money (division), opinion, 136–137
outsourcing, opinion, 145–146
people, issue, 125–126
profile, 196–197
ROI, opinion, 70
technology project audit, 92–93

H

Hankins, Steve, 43, 44, 59–62
business processes, opinion, 72–73
Carr article, opinion, 155, 158–159
governance, usage, 97
head counting, 123
payback/soft costs, 135–136
profile, 197
team leader, 89
technology, usage/forefront, 161
value, yardstick, 65–66
Heriot-Watt University, 170
Hewlett-Packard (HP), 67, 70, 161
Hupfeld, Stan, 34, 61–62
auditing, active program, 90
CIOs, types, 140–141
external auditing, value, 79
profile, 198

I

Ideas/viewpoints, usage, 167, 183–185
Information manipulation, 69
Information technology (IT), 213
application, 34
business
model, 137
operation, strategy, 132–136

partners, relationship, 74
units, relationship, 59–63
costs, 100–101
departments, 60
efforts, 59
expenditures, benefits, 87–88
improvement, 17
infrastructure support services, 29
issue, 62
organization, 18, 120, 144
revenue generation, 30
overcharging, 138
potential, 8
question, 63–64
responsibility, 13
role, 130–132
strategy, explanation (difficulty), 11–12
team, 14–15, 24
Information Work Productivity Council, 68–69
Infrastructure costs, competitive costs (contrast), 162–164
In-house customers, 99–100
Instant Messaging (IM), usage, 38, 164
Integris Health, 33–36
approach, 61–62
auditing, commitment, 90
board-level committee, 62
Capital Expenditures Committee, 63
CIO role, 140–141
IT, process automation, 35–36
standardization issues, 141–142
Interactive University (IU), 169–170, 195, 200
Internal audit department, 90
Internet connection, 27
Inventions, 153
reactions, 154–157

J

JetBlue Airways, 22–23, 193–194
  IT budget, 181
  standardization, 142
Jodie, S. Kregg, 8–9, 13
  Carr article, opinion, 158
  profile, 198
  technology management, 132–133
  value, opinion, 80–81
Joint Forces Command (JiffComm), 121
Joint ownership, advantage, 84

K

Kane, Archie, 16–17, 46
  auditing, insistence, 85–86
  IT discipline, 177
  processes, fixing, 177–178
  profile, 199
  strategies, building, 133–134
  technology projects, opinion, 90–91
Keystone Marketing Specialists, Inc., 147, 203–204
Killinger, Kerry, 4
Knowledge work, 69

L

Leadership
  impact, 3
  team, strategic backing, 9
Leitch, Roy, 169–170
  profile, 200
Lloyds Bank (Lloyds TSB), 16–17, 39–40, 46, 199
  audit process, impact, 85–86
  efficiency/productivity improvement efforts, 85
  technology projects, evaluation, 90–91
Loaiza, Jazmín, 183
  profile, 200

M

Management transition, 44
Marsh, Inc., 9–11, 63–64, 204
  business/strategic impact, 211–212
  colleague impact, 212
  Customer Relationship Management, 63
  governance
    council, composition, 98–99
    function, 106–110
  IT governance committee, 106
  IT project, approval, 107–108
  process impact, 212
  projects, 66–67
  technology
    governance, progress, 87–88
    project, initiation process, 172
  Technology Governance Template, usage, 211
  working groups, usage, 108–110
Mary Kay Inc., 13, 198
  culture change/IT change, 132–133
  value, gaining, 80–81
Maslow, Abraham (needs hierarchy), 144
McDowell, Bob, 207–208
Medicine, technology usage, 174–176
Meslow, Eric
  answers, difficulty, 148–149
  expenditure, opinion, 75–77
  information, centralization, 182–183
  profile, 200–201
  technology, priorities, 75
Microsoft, 67–70, 114, 129, 181
  CEO Summit, 68
Mileur, Rachelle, 23–25, 45
  commodity/infrastructure perspective, 154–155

governance, approach, 100–101
IT, strengths, 131
profile, 201
technology justification, 73–74
Mitnick, Kevin, 173
Moore, Gary, 52–54
outsourcing, opinion, 144–145
profile, 202
technology, capabilities,
102–103
Mui, Chunka, 117

N

Neeleman, David, 22
Negroponte, Nicholas, 117
NetMeeting, usage, 38
Non-critical activities, 47
Non-profit agencies, competitive
advantage, 29
Non-profit joint research effort, 69
Northeast power outage, 11

O

Outlook, usage, 38
Outsourcing, advantages/disadvan-
tages, 143–146

P

Performance, evaluation, 62–63
Per-piece arrangement, 30–31
Problems, awareness, 129
Productivity
academic viewpoint, 67–68
improvement
technology, usage, 33–41
third wave, 40
issues, efficiency, 67
measurement methods, 68–70
push, 36–40
Profit, motivation, 29
Push-pull exercise, 108

Q

Quick-hit deliverables, 4

R

Raikes, Jeff, 68
Reengineering, 46
Research and development (R&D)
organization, 37
Residential Capital Group, 6–7, 14,
98, 196
IT evolution, 130
Residential Funding Corporation
(RFC), 6–7, 14, 49, 130
Resistance, 80–84
Return on investment (ROI), 155,
213
usage, 70–72
Rootenberg, John, 174–176
profile, 202–203
Ruby slippers thinking, 129

S

SAP, 67, 70, 158
Schlenker, Lee, 67–68, 118, 153
profile, 203
viewpoints, 155
Scottish Widows, 16
Settle, Karen, 32–33, 147
profile, 203–204
technology dollars, exploitation,
149–150
Simon, Bill, 173, 208–209
Single owner concept, 60
Small business owner, characteristics, 32–33
Small company
audit, challenge, 91–92
competitive advantage, 26–27
experience, 18–20
IT, relationship, 146–150
ROI, impact, 74–77
technology, spending decisions,
74–77
Smith, Roger H., 9–11, 63–64
competitor, differentiation,
162–163

governance
    assistance, 103–105
    description, 98–99
    profile, 204
    project initiation, 179–181
    promises, 66–67
    ROI, opinion, 71
    surprises, 184
    technology
        governance, progress
            (description), 87
        understanding, 171–172
Social engineering, 173
Southwest Airlines,
    customer/employee experience,
    125–126
Sperry Rand, 89
Standardization, considerations,
    141–143
Success, budgeting, 136–138
Surround and conquer strategy, 44
Szpak, Terry, 26–27
    employees, support, 160–161
    profile, 204–205
    technology
        expenditures, business value
            audit, 91–92
        payoff, 74–75

T
Technology
    achievement, 3–6
    advice, 179–183
    application, 59. *See also* Business
    business case, making, 59, 79
    change, 52
    corporate leaders, relationship,
        16–18
    cost, justification, 59. *See also*
        Airborne
    deployment, 46
    education, relationship,
        168–171
    evolution, 47–49

    example, 186–189
    impact, 3. *See also* Business
    implementation, 97
    investment, perspective, 82–83
    justification, 43
    observations, 171–174
    ownership, transition, 63–65
    process
        application, 45–47
        fixing, 177–179
    projects, 55
        trouble, prevention, 49–50
    purchase, reasons, 21
    strategy, 8–9
    tactics, 179–183
    trailing edge, 47
    trust, 9–11
Telesystems West, 26–27, 204–205
Telesystems West technology
    advances, teaching, 149
    advantages, 160–161
    expenditures, business value
        audit, 91–92
    payoff, 74–75
Texaco, 68
    merger, 51, 103–105, 131, 178
Third-party company, 92
Timbercon, Inc., 200–201
    bank balance, 148–149
    expenditure, impact, 75–77
    technology
        passing, 182–183
        priorities, 75, 149
Time management/problem,
    167–168
Tracking information project, 73
Training, technology-based
    process, 52–54
Tyson Foods, 44, 59–62, 197
    business expansion, 134–136
    business-unit leaders, convinc-
        ing, 61–62
    company acquisition, 89
    executive head count, 123

governance, usage, 97
technology
    application, 72–73
    value, assessment, 65–66

U

Up front analyses, 82
U.S. Army, 6, 11–12, 192–193, 205
    automated identification technology, 54–55
    Business Initiatives Council, 55
    culture gap, 114–115
    Defense Logistics Agency
        (DLA), 64–65
    Enterprise Systems Technology
        Activity, 46
    NCO Corps, 125
    observations, 29
    ROI, impact, 71
    technology usage, 120–121
U.S. Bureau of Labor Statistics,
    information data, 69

V

Value
    achievement. *See* Business
    demonstration, 79
    measurement. *See* Business
Vendors, technology usage,
    161–162
Virtual Private Network (VPN), 4
Voice over IP, usage, 27, 160
von Bernewitz, Carla A., 6, 29, 54,
    114
    change, groundwork, 122–123
    guidelines, 65
    hold-back-the-dawn attitude,
        134
    legacy systems, 64
    philosophy, 118
    profile, 205
    standards, competition, 141
    systems/organizational change,
        121–122

W

Wachovia Corporation, 191
    business dynamics, 167–168
    company culture, 113–114
    discipline, 130
    eCommerce Division, 49–50
    governance, impact, 99–100
    ROI, impact, 72
Washington Mutual (WaMu), 3,
    16, 196–197
    auditing approach, 93–94
    Capital Expenditures (CapEx)
        Committee, 101–102
        process, 92–93
    governance, approach, 101–102
    IT function, monetization, 145
    leadership, 62–63
    model program, 92–93
    offshore questions, 185
    problems, 12
    process, 119
    ROI, 70
    standardization, disadvantage,
        142
    technology
        investments, spreading,
            136–137
        project audit, 92–93
Wilson, David, 18–20, 27–28,
    30–32
    backstory, 47–48
    business focus, 146–147
    profile, 205–206
Work Productivity Council, 194

1122